Anna Quindlen

THINKING

OUT

LOUD

On the Personal, the Political, the Public and the Private

Fawcett Columbine • New York

A Fawcett Columbine Book
Published by Ballantine Books

Library of Congress Catalog Card Number: 93-90547

ISBN: 0-449-90905-0

Cover design by Ruth Ross
Cover photo by Joyce Ravid

Manufactured in the United States of America

First Ballantine Books Edition: April 1994

10   9   8   7   6   5   4   3   2   1

Other Books by Anna Quindlen

Object Lessons*
Living Out Loud*
The Tree That Came to Stay (Children's book)

*Published by Ballantine Books

THINKING
OUT
LOUD

For Quindlen, Christopher, and Maria Krovatin

Had I the heavens' embroidered cloths,
Enwrought with golden and silver light,
The blue and the dim and the dark cloths
Of night and light and the half-light,
I would spread the cloths under your feet:
But I, being poor, have only my dreams;
I have spread my dreams under your feet;
Tread softly because you tread on my dreams.

—WILLIAM BUTLER YEATS

My advice to the women of America is to raise more hell and fewer dahlias.

—WILLIAM ALLEN WHITE

Acknowledgments

In 1988, when he was deputy publisher and I was preparing to leave *The New York Times* for the last time, Arthur Sulzberger, Jr., approached me about the possibility of becoming an Op-Ed-page columnist. He will always have my gratitude for that blessed leap of faith. So will Arthur O. Sulzberger, who made the formal offer, and Jack Rosenthal, who told me in no uncertain terms to take it.

Twice a week the best copy editors in the business vet my work. You don't see the names of Steve Pickering and Linda Cohn on my column, but their care and attention are in everything good I do.

My colleagues at *The New York Times* are the most generous people—and the finest reporters and editors—I could ever know. Those in the Washington and City Hall bureaus, on the national staff covering social policy and on the metro staff covering social welfare, know how often I have called upon them to share reporting and insight. They have been invaluable sources of information and inspiration.

All my friends have been involved with this column, but three deserve special notice. I owe a good deal to the wit and wisdom of the team of Michael Specter and Alessandra Stanley. And if Janet Maslin didn't exist, I would have had to invent her, so that I could have someone smart, thoughtful, and funny to talk to every morning on the phone.

Two books in particular have been of great help to me over these last three years, giving me a historical grounding in the work of opinion-column writing. The first, Charles Fisher's *The Columnists: A Surgical Survey,* was published in 1944. The second, Peter Kurth's superb biography of Dorothy Thompson, *American Cassandra,* put me in touch with the woman whose work first informed my own. Both were primary sources for the introduction to this book.

For three years Elizabeth Cohen has been much more than my assistant. She has been my surrogate, my protector, and my office voice. This is her book, too. And it also belongs to Amanda Urban, who is a great agent and a better friend, and Kate Medina, who is the best editor in the book business.

Quindlen, Christopher, and Maria Krovatin, my children, have been extraordinarily understanding of how distracted I can be, particularly on what are known around here as column days. And they have consistently provided me with good material—and a sane and balanced view of the world that I would not have had otherwise.

There's little precedent for a man married to an opinion columnist, since there have been and continue to be too few of us who are female. Sinclair Lewis, when he was married to pundit doyenne Dorothy Thompson, used to beg not to have It discussed in his home, It being the world situation or anything else that smacked of the Op-Ed page. My husband, Gerry Krovatin, has instead been unstinting of his opinions on every aspect of It, and uncomplaining if I did not adopt them. And he is responsible for what remains the best line in anything that has appeared with my byline: "Could you get up and get me a beer without writing about it?" I suppose this is the answer.

Contents

Acknowledgments   XI

"Altogether Female"—An Introduction   XVII

UNSOLICITED OPINIONS   1

The Old Block   6

A Changing World   9

The Great White Myth   12

Tyson Is Not Magic   15

To Defray Expenses   18

Across the Divide   21

Erin Go Brawl   24

No Closet Space   27

With Extreme Prejudice   30

Evan's Two Moms   33

Moving the Furniture Around   36

Room at the Inn   39

No Place Like Home   42

Somalia's Plagues   45

Seeking a Sense of Control   48
A Time to Die   51
Justice and Mercy   54
Parental Rites   57
Believe in Magic   60
Foul Play   63
Journalism 2001   66
Suffer the Little Children   69
A Mistake   72

KIDS AND ANIMALS   75
The Days of Gilded Rigatoni   81
Suicide Solution   84
Cradle to Grave   87
With Babies on Board   90
Rabbit Punch   94
Another Kid in the Kitchen   97
Men at Work   100
The Waiting List   103
Mom Alone   106
Babes in Toyland   109
Mommy Dimmest   112
Naughty and Nice   115
Enough Bookshelves   118
Mr. Smith Goes to Heaven   121

ON THE NEWS   125
Justice for the Next Century   131
The Blank Slate   134
Listen to Us   137
An American Tragedy   140
The Perfect Victim   143
The Trouble with Teddy   146
The Invasion Vacation   149
Summer's Soldiers   152
New World At War   155
The Questions Continue   158

In the Shadow of War 161
Personally 164
The Back Fence 167
The Domestic Front 170
Regrets Only 173
Reservations Not Accepted 176
The Microwave War 179
No There There 182
Just Say Yes 185
Advantage, Mr. Clinton 188
Gender Contender 191
All of These You Are 194
The Two Faces of Eve 197
The Fourth Wall 200
One View Fits All 203
Rumor Has It 206
A Place Called Hope 209

WOMEN'S RITES 213
The Abortion Account 219
Mom, Dad, and Abortion 222
The Nuns' Story 225
Offensive Play 228
Rust, Roe, and Reality 231
Hidden Agendas 234
The Abortion Orphans 237
At the Clinics 240
Hearts and Minds 243
One Vote 246
The Truth Telling 249
No More Waiting 252
Bears with Furniture 255
Dirt and Dignity 258
The Cement Floor 261
A Team Dream 264
Heroine Addiction 267
Rebels Without a Clue 270

Getting a Second Wind   273

Ms. President   276

Not about Breasts   279

Contradictions   282

The Glass Half Empty   285

"ALTOGETHER FEMALE"
—An Introduction

One afternoon in Denver a young reporter came to interview me about a novel I had written. But the talk soon turned to my opinion column in *The New York Times*, since, like half the young reporters in the business, this one wanted to be a columnist someday. (The other half want to be executive editor.) "But is it really necessary," he asked after some preliminaries, "for you to wear your gender on your sleeve?"

For a moment I thought about telling him where my gender really resided, but he seemed pleasant and earnest and I didn't want to embarrass him. Besides, although he'd worded it in a peculiar fashion, his question was one I'd been asked often, by colleagues, friends, critics, and readers. Truth to tell, it was a question I'd asked myself for a long, long time.

Half a century ago Dorothy Thompson, perhaps the best-known woman to fill a column of type on any paper's Op-Ed page, complained about being habitually told she had "the brains of a man." Her strength, she insisted, was "altogether female."

(Miss Thompson, who at the time was writing three columns a week, touring the lecture circuit, and being touted as the second most powerful woman in the country after Eleanor Roosevelt, laid it on a bit thick when she added, "I wish somebody would say that I am a hell of a good housewife, that the food by me is swell, that I am almost a perfect wife. . . .")

But her complaints underscore a question that has been with me since 1990, when I became the third woman to write a column on the *Times* Op-Ed page. Is it part of the modern mission of a woman columnist to be somehow overtly female in print?

The answer might not have been yes a half century ago, when Miss Thompson was assigned to produce a "cozy woman-to-woman chat," a "chat" that became one of the most influential columns in the country on the state of the world and the nation. And the answer may not be yes a half century from now, when the idea of gender specificity may seem quaint. My predecessors at *The New York Times,* Anne O'Hare McCormick and Flora Lewis, were both women with extraordinary expertise in geopolitics; they could have written under their first initials without any clue to their sex being contained within their copy. My successors might well be women who air their opinions in an atmosphere so egalitarian that making much of being a woman is superfluous.

But right here, right now, I believe it is not only possible but critical, not only useful but illuminating, for a woman writing an opinion column to bring to her work the special lens of her gender.

I am one of those people who have loved newspapers all their lives, loved the smell of them, the feel of them, especially loved the idea of all those reporters, out on the streets and at their desks and phones, discovering first what's what and whipping it, every day, into some coherent version of instant history. I love the chaos and the cacophony of newsrooms, with their barracks sprawl and utter lack of privacy. When I first started working at home, I was amused by the sympathy the arrangement evoked in people who said it must be so hard to write with kids around.

Trust me: a preschool is less noisy than a fair-sized city room any day of the week.

I grew up in the newspaper business, went from eighteen and covering demonstrations against the Vietnam War to thirty-one and visiting abortion clinics under siege. I was a city columnist when New York was in a period of extraordinary flux and an editor when the *Times* was in a period of flux too, trying to re-create itself in a changing market.

Those changes were good ones because, although I had long loved newspapers, even I had sometimes felt that the events contained in them were somehow other, the sort of things that happened to other people, the kinds of things about which the people we accost at the scenes of tragedies say, "I never thought something like this could happen to me." When I first began working in the newspaper business, I was hard-pressed to find myself between the pages of the papers for which I worked.

I don't mean my literal self: I believed then fervently in the idea that I was meant to be hidden from the reader, a byline without a face, a voyeur without a point of view. But I could not find approximations of my life, either. There were murders and Senate bills and press conferences and White House briefings and Vietnam casualties and Russian evasions. But those of us looking for reflections of our own lives, our problems and relationships and constant concerns, found them more often in fiction than in the daily newspaper. We women had a section of our own, supposedly, called the woman's section, but in small papers it seemed to consist largely of recipes, sewing patterns, and Dear Abby or Ann Landers, and in larger and more sophisticated newspapers there was a good deal about couture and the Beautiful People, the kind of people I had no opportunity or desire to meet.

Our dissatisfaction with the impersonality of newspapers was not a new phenomenon. In 1944 a writer named Charles Fisher derided that impersonality in a book called *The Columnists: A Surgical Survey*. The introduction argues that a newspaper once carried the personal stamp of its publisher but that that had changed. "The great portion of the American press has been congealed for years in a pattern which is admirably useful and impeccably dull," Mr. Fisher wrote. "There isn't much in most successful American newspapers to excite living interest, or affection, or dislike."

The lack of what would "excite living interest," noteworthy in 1944, had become critical forty years later because of great changes in journalism and in society. Mr. Fisher could argue that the EXTRA! that went out when great events took place had a homogenized sameness because of the caution of publishers and the rise of the wire services. But those of us in the business in the 1980s knew that that EXTRA! was often as worthy of an exclamation point as the weather report. Television beat us to so many of the biggest stories, just by being able to be there, with the few words and pictures it takes to communicate the simple existence of a space-shuttle explosion, a jury verdict, a death, a birth. The ascendancy of cable channels meant that news was on the air as it happened, twenty-four hours a day. Hampered by our deadlines, by the simple fact that a newspaper lands on most people's doorsteps a good twelve hours after the evening news, we tried to rise to each occasion with better in-depth coverage, more analysis and background, the kind of thing that time constraints usually demand that television do incompletely, if at all.

There was no doubt, at the tail end of the twentieth century, that newspapers were going to have to change. And part of that change was driven by a larger change in society. Fifty years ago America had its papers to tell it what Franklin Roosevelt and Adolf Hitler were doing, and what Walter Lippmann and Dorothy Thompson thought they ought to be doing. The country had back fences to discuss the shortcomings of children, the problems in marriage, the scandals down the street. Perhaps in the last ten years newspapers have become back fences for people, now that so many of the old back fences are gone.

Certainly *The New York Times* that I joined in 1977 is now a very

ALTOGETHER FEMALE / XXI

different newspaper. During my first fifteen years we added sections called "Living" and "Home," features on child rearing and
personal fitness, columns about what it felt like to be female and
what it felt like to be male. (It is testimony to how some of us felt
about the contents of the paper that when the "About Men" column was inaugurated, we whispered, "Why? The whole paper is
about men.") There are still jokes that the computers automatically obliterate adjectives, but the truth is that there are more
adjectives than ever before. Readers needed something different
from us than we had once given them in the who-what-when-
where-why days. We tried to provide it.

I felt the change most keenly when I worked out a long maternity leave after the birth of my second child by signing on to write
a column called "Life in the 30s." In his book, Charles Fisher suggests that the rise of the newspaper pundit—and it is difficult to
overestimate how powerful and influential people like Miss
Thompson, Mr. Lippmann and others like them were during
their heyday—was an attempt to give a determinedly human
voice to journalism gone bland as tapioca. The column I wrote
for three years was, no doubt about it, written in a determinedly
female voice, and it was considerably off the usual news. In some
ways its very existence mirrored the changes in our business.

While my colleagues on the Op-Ed page were dissecting the
Reagan administration, the state of the Soviet Union, and the
state of the National League, I was writing about our two young
sons and the world contained within the four walls of our house.
Alice Roosevelt Longworth once described Dorothy Thompson
as "the only woman in history who has had her menopause in
public and made it pay." On a much smaller scale, I did the same
with my kids. It was a wonderful opportunity to combine work
and family, work I was proud of and a family that eventually grew
to three young children. And it was an opportunity for the paper
to make a statement, too, to show readers that amid the foreign
news, the stock market tables and the television reviews there was
room for one woman's thoughts on the quieter moments. When

people would carp about taking up space in *The New York Times* with my memories of Halloween, I had a flippant reply: "They didn't cut back the Moscow bureau for this." What I meant was that we could be all things to all people, and that there were great things taking place in our kitchens as well as in the Kremlin. This justified my professional existence, but I also believed it, believed that if newspapers were going to survive and thrive in a television age they were going to have to use their gift of words in ways they had not considered before.

I found the relentless self-exposure of "Life in the 30s" wearing, and in some ways it was a great relief, packing it in after three years, being able to be with my children without thinking Can I use that? when one of them said something telling. I wrote the last column the week after our daughter, Maria, was born, and it ended with the words "Sometimes it is time to examine your life. And sometimes it is time to just live it. Today I embrace the unexamined life. . . ." And I meant it.

And then I was offered an Op-Ed page column, perhaps the best job *The New York Times* has to offer one of its writers. The unexamined life went into the storage closet with Maria's stretchies and crib sheets.

There were many reasons to want this job, but the fact that I am a woman was not inconsequential. When I first interviewed for a job as a reporter at the *Times,* fifteen years ago, the managing editor, a kind, rather dolorous-looking man with wavy hair the color of pewter, asked me what my ambition was. I said I wanted to be a general-assignment reporter, one of that great mass of people assigned to no one thing in particular, called up to the desk whenever a plane crashes or a pol speaks or an editor simply has a brilliant idea.

Yes, he said, he understood that that was the job I was interviewing for, but what did I ultimately want to do? It occurred to me that, for some reason, being a city reporter was not considered a worthy ambition in this big building on Forty-third Street. Remembering the biographical material about him that I'd read the night before, I said that I wanted to be Bonn bureau chief, Germany having been one of his foreign assignments. His face lit up. "How is your German?" he asked. "Not great," I replied, since the only German I knew consisted of the names of casserole dishes. When he passed me on to the executive editor, I told *him* I wanted to cover Poland; I knew he had won his Pulitzer in War- saw.

For some months I thought my clever duplicity and my prose accounted for my job offer, since I was in no way a *Times*man, being twenty-four, relatively inexperienced, and, of course, a woman. And then at some point I got it; I realized that that was exactly why I had gotten hired in the first place—because I was a woman.

That fact has shaped my life at the *Times* ever since. It has affected the responsibilities I feel toward my colleagues, toward the paper and its readers.

In 1974 six women at the *Times* brought a class-action suit against the paper, charging that women were not being paid, hired, or promoted in parity with men. Between that time and the time the suit was settled in 1978, the *Times* hired a number of women in all departments, including me. While the collective memory of those events faded as the years went on, except in the minds of those who were courageous enough to bring the suit in the first place, the effects remained for women in general and for me in particular. In 1981, when I became the first woman to write the "About New York" column on a regular basis, and again in 1983, when I became deputy metropolitan editor, the first woman in that position, I was keenly aware that I was the beneficiary of other people's courage.

But when I began to write "Life in the 30s" I became aware of something else, something that marked a great shift in the women's movement during its second decade. And that was the difference, in all businesses as well as in my own, between the choices made by men and women.

I don't simply mean in the more obvious ways, although I knew that my decision to ditch a promising management career because I had two children in two years was seen as distinctly—and incredibly—female. I mean in more everyday attitudes. Like some of my female colleagues, I was more interested in writing about the small moments in people's lives than in covering a presidential press conference. Like some of my female colleagues, I found standard journalistic forms limited, even though those hard-news page-one stories were often the stuff of which advancement was made.

It was a chicken-egg argument—after all, many of us had long been relegated to covering the small moments, the color instead of the news; many of us had been placed in back-of-the-book positions where a more literary style and looser construction were tolerated. In our determination during the seventies to be treated equally, we wanted to be sent to cover the White House, the Supreme Court, the wars. But as time went by we began to feel freer to discuss differences within the context of being treated fairly and equitably. We began to admit that some of what we had once covered about home and hearth still moved us as reporters, that we believed writing about those matters was as important for readers as the world events we had been offering them on page one.

What happened to women in the newspaper business is what happened to women in so many other places, too. Once we stood shoulder to shoulder with our male colleagues we decided that some of what they did was tedious and some of it was ill conceived. The Supreme Court was an interesting beat, but not if you didn't know much about the character, alliances, and backgrounds of the men and woman who served as Supreme Court justices. The White House required more than covering press conferences. It required a sense of texture, of personality, of the personal interplay that no press-conference coverage provides.

The irony of the role of women in my business, and in so many other places, too, was that while we began by demanding that we be allowed to mimic the ways of men, we wound up knowing we would have to change those ways. Not only because those ways were not like ours, but because they simply did not work. The newspapers that Mr. Fisher described as dull and homogenized in 1944 were written overwhelmingly by white men, for white men, and so they did not reflect the communities or the concerns of so many of us. And they were written to a formula that said the facts were the only thing. In our hearts and our minds, too, we knew that simply wasn't so.

If male was hard news and female was features—and in many papers, for a long time, that was exactly how matters of gender broke down—the newspapers of the twenty-first century would clearly have to be more female. Less other, more back fence. Either that, or they would perish in the twenty-four-hour glow of the television screen.

I thought a good deal about all of this when I became an Op-Ed-page columnist and had to decide how I would fit in among the six distinguished male journalists with whom I shared the page. I carried with me a legacy from "Life in the 30s," and it was overwhelmingly a legacy of criticism. The feeling about that column on the part of some of my colleagues was that it was too personal, too particular, and too stereotypically feminine—that is, too obsessed with child rearing and relationships. I had strayed a long way from a notion of objectivity which said that the reader should know no more about me than my name. I now had readers who knew how much weight I'd gained during my pregnancies and what I wore to bed at night.

I was not going to reprise that on the Op-Ed page, a place in the paper that took itself a good deal more seriously than the style section in which my previous column had appeared. But if the notion of objectivity seemed suspect to me even in news stories, it seemed preposterous in an opinion column. In this line of work, biography is destiny. It would not serve the reader if William Safire pretended he had not once worked in the Nixon White House; instead he uses his memories and connections from those days to bring us some of the best columns that appear on the page.

An undeniable part, perhaps the largest part of my biography, is that I am a woman. Would it serve the reader for me to write about abortion without having as my underlying premise the fact that I could be, in fact had been, pregnant? Would it serve to talk about parental leave legislation without bringing to the discussion, tacitly or overtly, the fact that I am a working mother? I did not think so.

But as time went by I realized the issues raised by a world view largely shaped by gender went deeper than that. The standard view of the columnist is of the Voice of God, intoning the last word on any subject: Capital punishment is wrong. Abortion is a woman's right. The point is the conclusion. This seems to me essentially uninteresting, this preaching to the converted, this emphasis on product rather than on process. From the beginning it seemed to me that the point was not to make readers think like me. It was to make them think.

Some readers thought this was stereotypically female, a gender-based avoidance of strong opinions, while others thought that my use of personal vignettes to make a point about public policy was unseemly and even bad for women. In other words, the standard set by male columnists, which had for many years been one that eschewed both doubt and the introduction of the personal into the political arena, was to be the standard set for all. Never mind that that standard was in conflict with the real world, where most of our readers had conflicting and confusing opinions about cutting-edge issues and brought their personal experiences almost automatically to their considerations of public policy. That was merely human; the columnist was to be somehow super-human, preternaturally sure of himself, unusually able to separate his view of the world and the world of his home.

But even when I had strong opinions and left my children out of them, there were those who thought they were inevitably connected with my sex, and perhaps they were right. There was the reader who hated my pacifist columns in opposition to the Gulf war. "If you were a real man," he wrote, "you'd understand why we need to be there." On the other hand, being a real woman was invaluable in certain situations. During the Anita Hill hearings, charges of sexual harassment in high places and the gender blindness of the United States Senate cried out not for a purely intellectual response but for righteous indignation as well, and for a feminist perspective. It seems to me that a dry intellectual discussion of a rape case on my part not only would be boring but would be, in some clear sense, a lie. There are issues about which I not only think but also feel. And yet standard operating procedure has been to bring the mind but not the heart to the table of public discourse. I had to wonder why. Is thought always more telling than emotion? Is the territory of the heart always secondary to that of the mind?

Or is it possible that we devalue certain ways of looking at the world because we have come to believe, for whatever reason, that those ways are the purview of women?

And what would it mean if six women brought a lawsuit against their newspaper for equality, and one of the visible results of that lawsuit was a woman doing a bad imitation of a man twice a week on the Op-Ed page?

When I was a girl my admiration for Dorothy Thompson had something to do with the fact that she wrote her column in bed, drinking black coffee, and dictating to a secretary. But when I reread her columns as a grown woman far less enamored of working in a supine position, what struck me was her willingness to write about the Third Reich one day and her nasturtiums the next. There is no contradiction between her power, her influence, her breadth of knowledge and interest, and her contention that she was "altogether female." Clearly she had settled the issue of emotion vs. intellect within her own mind. Of a collection of her columns entitled *Let the Record Speak*, one reviewer wrote, "Dorothy Thompson writes fierily. Sometimes she seems to write almost hysterically. . . . She gets mad. She pleads; she denounces. And the result is that where the intellectualized columns of her colleagues fade when pressed between the leaves of a book, these columns still ring."

In a speech in 1939 she said:

"One cannot exist today as a person—one cannot exist in full consciousness—without having to have a showdown with one's self, without having to define what it is that one lives by, without being clear in one's own mind what matters and what does not matter." They were words of clear guidance for me from a more experienced woman when I began to write the Op-Ed column we named "Public & Private."

Now, three years later, the words that speak loudest to me are much simpler, less lofty, perhaps, in their bread-and-butter tone, more stereotypically "altogether female." In a letter Dorothy Thompson's son received after her death in 1961, the last sentence was "As I write this little note, I feel very grateful." Me, too: for all the women who laid the groundwork. These are my words; this is their world, a world in which we can wear our gender on our sleeves, unabashedly, as we go about the business of thinking out loud.

UNSOLICITED
OPINIONS

A t a dinner mourning his retirement, Tom Wicker, who had been a columnist at the *Times* for a quarter century, read a letter he'd received that day from a reader: "1992 is shaping up to be a good year. First we got rid of Gorbachev and now we're getting rid of you."

We laugh at the mail from readers that suggests that we are mistaken, ill informed, or are just plain idiots. And yet I find it inescapable, and telling, too, that the letters I receive from readers that are strongest in every way—powerfully moving as well as horribly insulting—are the ones that come as the result of columns about those issues I've embraced most passionately.

It has always seemed to me that this bully

pulpit should devote itself, in large part, to those who have no pulpit at all, to the publicly disfranchised. While I care about the affairs of the White House, Congress, and the world community, there are many more people to speak for and about them than there are to speak for the powerless, whether it be the homeless, the poor, the gay men and lesbians, African-Americans, the terminally ill, or people with AIDS. I have chosen often to write about those people and their problems. And the response has often been discouraging.

I don't mean that all the mail is brickbats. I remember the day my assistant called to say, "You got a fan letter from Paul Simon!" It was only later that I realized I didn't know whether it was the singer or the senator. (It was the senator.) When I won the Pulitzer Prize in 1992, I was often asked what the best thing about it was. The honest answer is that everything about winning the Pulitzer is great. But the thing I found most cheering was the mail from perfect strangers (emphasis on the adjective) who took time out to say: Congratulations. We are pleased and proud. I kept all those letters, and when I'm getting clobbered pretty badly I'll read one or two.

Because part of this job is getting clobbered with some regularity. In my case, the columns that generate the most mail tend to be the ones about those social-welfare issues that move me most powerfully. The response to those issues never ceases to amaze me: the meanness, the vitriol, the Old Testament verses, the Ku Klux Klan literature. With the exception of abortion, I receive no mail on any issue that is as horrid and ignorant as the mail I get on gay rights. (While I have received a fair number of passionate, intelligent, deeply thoughtful letters about why abortion is wrong, I have yet to receive such a letter about homosexuality.) I will never understand people who think that the way to show their righteous opposition to sexual freedom is to write letters full of filthy words. Nor do I understand people like the man who thought the way to show us what he thought of the idea of gay people serving in the military was to send a box of dead roaches. And by first-class mail, too.

But the flip side of all this comes when you give voice to people who feel rendered mute by the great world. They are grateful out of all proportion to the simple act.

I was prepared to be reviled for suggesting that gay Irish should be given a place in the St. Patrick's Day parade, and I was. ("It's a good thing her grandfather's already dead," one caller said the day the column appeared, "or she would have killed him for sure this morning.") But I was not prepared for the letters of gratitude from so many gay people. I was prepared for negative mail about an affirmative action column. But I was not prepared for all the mail from African-Americans who said, "Thank you for speaking our truth."

I was unprepared for the reaction we got when I wrote about the press itself, about how and why we do what we do. Clearly the readers believed we never considered such things, when in fact it sometimes seems that considering them is most of what we do. This was particularly true of what became, for a while, my best-known column, a piece criticizing *The New York Times* for its coverage of the woman who had accused William Kennedy Smith of raping her in Palm Beach. (Mr. Smith, of course, was later acquitted of those charges and the woman, Patricia Bowman, went public to insist that what she had said was true. But before and during the trial the question of using her name was of great moment.) I made the mistake of going on vacation soon after that column, and several readers called to ask whether I had been fired. One right-wing zealot thought that after months of championing welfare cheats, boozy vagrants, and perverts I had finally gotten my just deserts. "Quindlen," he wrote with glee, like Tom Wicker's New Year's correspondent, "you are out of there!"

We laugh about the mail. But some of it still stings me—until I recall the balm. When you write about the parents of gay people and a young man writes to say that he used the column as a way of coming out to his mother and father—well, you can get by on something like that for a long, long time.

THE OLD BLOCK

May 17, 1992

The block on which my father grew up half a century ago is a truncated little street that leads nowhere. If it were a foot or two narrower, the map makers might have called it an alley. The houses are identical two-story attached brick buildings with bay windows on the top floor, an overobvious attempt at grandeur.

In this quiet backwater in the southwestern part of the city the children of Irish-Catholic families played in the late afternoons after they had changed from their parochial school uniforms. A police officer walked by twice a day, talking to the people he knew so well.

My father remembers that in one fifteen-minute span when he was eight years old he was hit by four people to whom he was not related: the cop; the neighbor whose window he drew upon with spit; the priest who saw him messing with a statue, and the nun who saw the priest whack him and wanted to second the emotion. So he grew.

Today the kids on the block are black. The house where the

seven Quindlen children were raised, the boys packed two to a bed, has long been empty. The small setback porch is still covered with debris from the fire that gutted the building several years ago. There is plywood nailed over the glassless windows and the doorless doorway.

This was a prosperous neighborhood, a way station to something better. Today it is a poor one, a dead end. Charred interiors are common. So are crime, drugs, and a sense of going nowhere.

Since L.A. burst into flames we have cast a net of blame in our search for those who abandoned America's cities.

The answer is simple. We did. Over my lifetime prosperity in America has been measured in moving vans, backyards and the self-congratulatory remark "I can't remember the last time I went to the city." America became a circle of suburbs surrounding an increasingly grim urban core.

In the beginning there was a synergy between the two; we took the train to the city to work and shop, then fled as the sun went down. But by the 1970s we no longer needed to shop there because of the malls. And by the 1980s we no longer had to work there because of the now-you-see-it rise of industrial parks and office complexes. Pseudo-cities grew up, built of chrome, glass, and homogeneity. Half of America now lives in the 'burbs.

We abandoned America's cities.

Ronald Reagan and George Bush did, too, and so did many Democrats, truth be told. And they're going to have to ante up now. But it's not enough anymore to let those boys take all the responsibility. They don't carry it well enough.

I understand how Eugene Lang felt when he gave a speech at his old grade school and, overwhelmed by the emptiness of words, offered all the students in the class a chance to go to college. I've heard the argument that Mr. Lang's largesse takes government off the hook. But I bet it's not compelling for kids who might have gone down the drain if one man hadn't remembered where he came from, before he moved on to someplace greener, richer, better.

Over the years I've heard about sister-city programs between places here and places abroad, places like Minsk or Vienna. Pen pals. Cultural exchange. Volunteer philanthropy. And all the while, twenty minutes away from the suburbs are cultures and lives and problems about which we are shamefully ignorant. I like the sister-city concept. Short Hills and Newark. South-central L.A. and Simi Valley. Both sides benefit.

The pols will lose interest in the cities again soon enough, because so many city residents are poor and powerless and not white. It would be nice to think of Congress as the home of idealists, but thinking like that makes you feel awfully foolish. America's cities will prosper when America's prosperous citizens demand it. When they remember their roots.

I've walked many times down blocks like the one on which my father grew up. I've been a poverty tourist with a notebook, but I never felt ashamed of it until now.

On that little street were the ghosts of the people who brought me into being and the flesh-and-blood kids who will be my children's companions in the twenty-first century. You could tell by their eyes that they couldn't figure out why I was there. They were accustomed to being ignored, even by the people who had once populated their rooms. And as long as that continues, our cities will burst and burn, burst and burn, over and over again.

A CHANGING
WORLD

May 20, 1990

These are dark days for the boys of Bensonhurst. Their world is fading as fast as the summer sun over the city some of their fathers and grandfathers helped build. They are angry the way people are angry when they see a sure thing slipping through their fingers.

Life was easier a generation ago. They graduated from high school, or maybe they didn't. It didn't really matter, because someone from the family or the neighborhood could get them into the union or the civil service, could find them a job working construction or picking up trash.

A couple of blocks away would be the girl, pretty, with hair and eyes as dark as the subway tunnels, and then there would be the wedding, and later the kids. She would serve dinner on a tray table in front of the television if the game was on, or keep it warm if the boys wanted to get together to play a little ball. She did shirts just right. Looking good was the thing when the day's grime was scrubbed away.

That has not changed. Looking good is still important. Keith Mondello never had a hair out of place during his trial. Just looking at him you could hear the blow dryer going. Joey Fama was found guilty of murder. Keith Mondello beat the big charges but was convicted of being part of a riot. When the riot was over, a black kid named Yusuf Hawkins was dead on the Bensonhurst sidewalk. They said afterward that it ruined the Feast of Santa Rosalia.

The people of Bensonhurst will tell you the boys were protecting the neighborhood. Common sense will tell you that it doesn't take forty guys with baseball bats to protect a city street from four teenagers looking to buy a used car. It doesn't take a gun.

Maybe what they were after wasn't Yusuf Hawkins at all but everything he represented. The lives the boys of Bensonhurst were banking on are as dead as Drexel Burnham Lambert, and for some of the same reasons. They liked to think they were tops in their neighborhood, and their neighborhood was tops in the city, and the city was the greatest in America, and America was the leader of the world.

All ashes.

America limps along, a superpower that, like a star high-school athlete grown middle-aged, ate too much but didn't exercise. It carries a paunch of second-rateness.

The girls that were once compliant talk back. They go out to work, and some of them even like it. The jobs aren't there anymore. The boys don't like to talk of slow housing starts or municipal cutbacks. They talk of how the jobs were all given away to blacks and Hispanics. Last week in Bensonhurst one of the delis put a picture of a watermelon in the window.

While the trial was going on, a study was released showing that, after blacks and Hispanics, Italian kids are most likely to drop out of school in New York. This came as a surprise to academia, but not to Bensonhurst. The kids who go to college move away, from the neighborhood and from their families, and that's no good.

When you say these things people will say you are anti-Italian, but ethnicity is beside the point. The boys of Bensonhurst have cousins all over America, from Irish-American boys in parts of Boston to good old boys in small towns down South. They were given to understand that they were better, not because they were smart or capable, but just because they were white men in a world that hated anyone who wasn't.

And then the world changed. But they didn't.

A black kid died in Bensonhurst, and someone killed him. You could argue that the whole block did it, although Mayor Dinkins refused to countenance group guilt. But these are places where people keep watch on the street, and as surely as someone is going to give my kids hell if they step off the curb on my block, someone watched the mob and they've kept quiet about it all this time. And they always will. This is the code of the boys, wherever they live: Take care of your own. No matter what.

Keeping the code, and the illusion of superiority, becomes harder every day. The economy is in the toilet, buying a house seems forever out of reach, and even when you get a job, you turn around and the guy next to you is black.

Yusuf Hawkins died fast on the pavement. The world of the boys of Bensonhurst, the world they try to protect by any means possible, will waste away and die more slowly. But it will not survive to convince another generation of its own superiority, an illusory arrogance that someone thought worth killing for.

THE GREAT WHITE MYTH

January 15, 1992

In a college classroom a young white man rises and asks about the future. What, he wants to know, can it possibly hold for him when most of the jobs, most of the good positions, most of the spots in professional schools are being given to women and, most especially, to blacks?

The temptation to be short, sarcastic, incredulous in reply is powerful. But you have to remember that kids learn their lessons from adults. That's what the mother of two black children who were sprayed with white paint in the Bronx said last week about the assailants, teenagers who called her son and daughter "nigger" and vowed they would turn them white. "Can you imagine what they are being taught at home?" she asked.

A nation based on laws, we like to believe that when they are changed, attitudes will change along with them. This is naive. America continues to be a country whose people are obsessed with maintaining some spurious pecking order. At the bottom are African-Americans, taught at age twelve and fourteen through the utter humiliation of having their faces cleaned with paint thinner that there are those who think that even becoming white from a bottle is better than not being white at all.

Each generation finds its own reasons to hate. The worried young white men I've met on college campuses in the last year have internalized the newest myth of American race relations, and it has made them bitter. It is called affirmative action, a.k.a. the systematic oppression of white men. All good things in life, they've learned, from college admission to executive position, are being given to black citizens. The verb is ubiquitous: given.

Never mind that you can walk through the offices of almost any big company and see a sea of white faces. Never mind that with all that has been written about preferential treatment for minority law students, only about 7,500 of the 127,000 students enrolled in law school last year were African-American. Never mind that only 3 percent of the doctors in this country are black.

Never mind that in the good old days preferential treatment was routinely given to brothers and sons of workers in certain lines of work. Perceptions of programs to educate and hire more black citizens as, in part, an antidote to decades of systematic exclusion have been inflated to enormous proportions in the public mind. Like hot-air balloons, they fill up the blue sky of the American landscape with the gaudy stripes of hyperbole. Listen and you will believe that the construction sites, the precinct houses, the investment banks are filled with African-Americans.

Unless you actually visit them.

The opponents of affirmative action programs say they are opposing the rank unfairness of preferential treatment. But there was no great hue and cry when colleges were candid about wanting to have geographic diversity, perhaps giving the kid from Montana an edge. There has been no national outcry when legacy applicants whose transcripts were supplemented by Dad's alumnus status—and cash contributions to the college—were admitted over more qualified comers. We somehow discovered that life was not fair only when the beneficiaries happened to be black.

And so the chasm widens. The old myth was the black American incapable of prosperity. It was common knowledge that welfare was purely a benefits program for blacks; it was common knowledge although it was false. The percentage of whites on public assistance is almost identical with the percentage of blacks.

The new myth is that the world is full of black Americans prospering unfairly at white expense, and anecdotal evidence abounds. The stories about the incompetent black co-worker always leave out two things: the incompetent white co-workers and the talented black ones. They also leave out the tendency of so many managers to hire those who seem most like themselves when young.

"It seems like if you're a white male you don't have a chance," said another young man on a campus where a scant 5 percent of his classmates were black. What the kid really means is that he no longer has the edge, that the rules of a system that may have served his father well have changed. It is one of those good-old-days constructs to believe it was a system based purely on merit, but we know that's not true. It is a system that once favored him, and others like him. Now sometimes—just sometimes—it favors someone different.

TYSON
IS NOT MAGIC

February 9, 1992

Consider the case of two champions. Both are the best at what they do; both are black. And both are considered heroes to kids in communities that sorely lack them. Magic Johnson is the one who has taught young men to use condoms. Mike Tyson is the one who has taught them to use women.

Mr. Tyson is on trial in Indianapolis, charged with raping a contestant in a black beauty pageant. People line up to shake his hand as he enters the courtroom, his atomic torso packed into a fine suit. He gets millions of dollars for doing within the perimeter of a ring what in the real world brings you an assault charge. This must be confusing.

People say his eighteen-year-old accuser is a gold digger, that a man so sought after by women need not force anyone to submit to him. Such a remark not only confuses sex and rape but ignores the central fact of Tyson's life: his profession is aggression. His trial is, inexplicably, being covered in the sports sections of many papers, as though it were just another bout. Perhaps that is how he sees it. Perhaps that is how he saw the night in question: I got her on the ropes now.

The Tyson trial brings to mind the prosecution of William Kennedy Smith, who was acquitted of rape in Palm Beach. There is the same bedrock suggestion that a woman who goes to a private spot with a man in the early morning hours should know that sexual contact is inevitable and any story of force incredible.

Mr. Smith's lawyer, Roy Black, has predicted that Mr. Tyson will be acquitted and has said he would have liked to defend him. (At a bar-association luncheon he also added that Mr. Smith's testimony describing two sexual encounters within a half hour had "helped him with dates," illustrating that an attorney must have many skills, but having good taste need not be among them.) Part of the Smith defense was that his behavior was perhaps caddish but not criminal. Mr. Tyson's lawyers have taken this even further. They suggest that their client is such a notorious lech that any woman who goes near him knows the risks.

I've got only eight hundred words, so I can't recount all reported Tyson maulings. There was the woman from Queens who said he grabbed and propositioned her in a nightclub, the ex-wife who said he beat her, and the lawyer who was reportedly told during a deposition exactly what he wanted to do to her, complete with hand gestures.

At the Miss Black America event at which Mr. Tyson met the alleged victim, one contestant said Mr. Tyson was like "an octopus," and the organizer, J. Morris Anderson, became famous overnight for characterizing Mr. Tyson as "a serial buttocks fondler." But Mr. Anderson did not pursue a lawsuit against the fighter, saying he had "second thoughts about participating in the crucifixion of a black role model."

Why in the world should Mike Tyson, a man who apparently can't pass a ladies' room without grabbing the doorknob, be a role model? Whether he raped anybody or not, it's clear he has disrespected black women from one end of this country to the other, as though they were hamburger and he were hungry. The cheerleader-cum-Sunday-school-teacher who says he raped her, so young that she refers to the way she felt afterward as "yucky," said she pleaded with him that she had a real future, that she was going to college. She says Mr. Tyson replied, "So, we have a baby," and then raped her without using a condom.

In that alleged exchange you have the choices in the lives of thousands of poor kids in this country. College. Baby. Condom. Future. The role model is supposed to be the person who points you toward the right one.

Every day those kids can watch Mike Tyson stride into the courtroom on the evening news, and they can see the middle-aged white women touch his hand, as though he were Wayne Newton or Elvis come back from the dead. And the message of Magic, the message that you have to make something of yourself, be responsible, face your mistakes, be a gentleman, will fade. The kids in poor neighborhoods, like the one in Brooklyn where Mike Tyson was once a street punk, have already learned from the drug dealer on the corner what Mr. Tyson has to teach: that if you're rich and dress well, you can do what you want. At least until you go to jail. Or until you're washed up. Here is the difference: Magic will never be washed up. In all the ways that truly matter, Mike Tyson already is.

TO DEFRAY
EXPENSES

March 1, 1992

> They are the children who fall out of their perambulators
> when the nurse is looking the other way. If they are not
> claimed in seven days they are sent far away to the Neverland
> to defray expenses.

The Lost Boys made news. The television crews and the newspaper reporters went to that Neverland called East New York to take note of the fact that one of them, aged fifteen, had allegedly shot and killed two others in a high school hallway in what classmates called a "beef." This means a disagreement.

It could have been Bushwick or the South Bronx or any of the other New York neighborhoods that are shorthand for going nowhere. It could have been Chicago or L.A. or any one of dozens of other cities. The Lost Boys are everywhere. Most especially in prison. By then, unlike the children Peter Pan described, they have grown up.

We reporters won't stay long. The Lost Boys claim public attention for only a short time, and many of us are loath to walk in their neighborhoods, which makes us no different from the people who live in them. The mayor was at the high school the day of the killings. He came to tell the students that they, too, could build a future. For many of them, the future is that short period of time between today and the moment when they shoot or get shot.

Homicide is the leading cause of death for black teenagers in America.

There is a lot of talk now about metal detectors and gun control. Both are good things. But they are no more a solution than forks and spoons are a solution to world hunger. Kids, particularly kids who live amid crack houses and abandoned buildings, have a right to think of their school as a safe haven. But it's important to remember that a kid can get himself a box cutter and wait outside until the last bell rings. With a metal detector, you can keep the homicide out of the hallways. Perhaps with something more, you can keep the homicide out of the heart.

"These boys die like it's nothing," said Angela Burton, whose boyfriend was one of the two killed in East New York.

The problem is that when we look into this abyss, it goes so deep that we get dizzy and pull back from the edge. Teenage mothers. Child abuse. Crowded schools. Homes without fathers. Projects lousy with drugs, vermin, crime. And, always, the smell of urine in the elevator. I have never been in a project that hasn't had that odor, and I have never smelled it without wondering, If your home smells like a bathroom, what does that tell you about yourself?

One of the ways to motivate kids is to say that if you do this bad thing now, you won't be able to do this good thing tomorrow. That doesn't work with the Lost Boys. They stopped believing in tomorrow a long time ago. The impulse control of an adolescent, the conviction that sooner or later you'll end up dead or in jail anyhow, and a handgun you can buy on the corner easier than getting yourself a pair of new Nikes: the end result is preordained.

"If you don't got a gun, you got to get one," said one teenager hanging with his friends at the corner of East New York and Pennsylvania Avenues.

If news is sometimes defined as aberration, as Man Bites Dog, it's the successes we should be rushing out to cover in these neighborhoods, the kids who graduate, who get jobs, who stay clean. Dr. Alwyn Cohall, a pediatrician who runs four school-based clinics in New York, remembers the day he was giving one of those kids a college physical, which is the happiest thing he ever does, when from outside he heard the sound. Pow. Pow. One moment he was filling out the forms for a future, the next giving CPR to another teenager with a gunshot wound blossoming in his chest. The kid died on the cement.

"He never even made the papers next day," the doctor recalled.

The story in East New York will likely end with the funerals. A fifteen-year-old killer is not that unusual; many city emergency rooms provide coloring books on gun safety. Dr. Cohall says that when the students at his schools come back after the long hot summer, they are routinely asked by the clinic staff how many of their friends were shot over vacation. The good doctor knows that it is possible to reclaim some of the Lost Boys, but it requires money, dedication, and, above all, the will to do it. Or we can continue to let them go. To defray expenses.

ACROSS
THE DIVIDE

May 3, 1992

They say that one way the defense attorneys won the case was by playing that videotape over and over, freezing the frames so that after a while it was no more than a random collection of points of light, highlighting the movements of the suspect instead of the batons of the police.

But no matter how many times I watch the four police officers beat up Rodney King, it still looks indefensible to me, and to the eight-year-old, too. Three times he watched the videotape and three times he brought his arms over his head in a double arch, as though to ward off baton blows. And finally he said, "Are they really allowed to do that?" It broke my heart, but it could have been worse. I pictured a mother and an eight-year-old watching the same clip, both of them black, the son asking the same question, the mother forced to reply, "Yes, baby, they are." The lawyers told the jurors that they had to pay attention to what happened before the videotape started rolling. Here's what came before: Ronald Reagan, Willie Horton, rotten schools, no jobs, falling plaster, broken boilers, David Duke. Years and years of rage and racism, measured now in angry words and broken glass.

Everyone wants to attack the jurors. Let's be honest, white folks: They walked into that room with the baggage most of us carry, the baggage of stereotypes and ignorance and pure estrangement from African-Americans. They walked in from a world that thinks the cops are the DMZ between us and them. And the defense made the most of it.

It makes you wonder whether the jury system, that bedrock of our society, can truly work when there is a fissure in our foundation so deep that sense disappears into it. It makes you wonder how many others could say, as one of the King jurors did the other night on television, that it didn't seem particularly significant that, just before the beating, one of the cops in the case said he'd had a call to a black household that was "right out of *Gorillas in the Mist.*" In some of our kids' schools they do this sensitivity exercise in which the blue-eyed kids treat the brown-eyed kids like garbage for the day. But at the end of the day lots of the brown-eyed kids go back to being just white kids with brown eyes. They move back across a deep divide. We wore ribbons to show our support for the hostages; we wear ribbons to show our concern for AIDS. I wondered about ribbons to repulse racism and then thought about how naive I was, on my side of the divide, as I watched Los Angeles burn.

It's as naive as thinking that because African-Americans go to Harvard and sit in the next booth at Burger King, it cancels out the neon sign that blinks NIGGER in white minds. It was rich with irony, that the fires raged as the last episode of *Cosby* was aired, the sitcom that let white America believe that being black was as easy as being brown-eyed, that their lives were just like ours except that their sweaters were better.

Somebody's daughter was on the news from Howard University, and she said that we had lied to her, that her parents and all the rest of us had given the impression that while racism still existed, it was no longer legal. But the Rodney King verdict taught her different. So smart. So sad. Even George Bush was wondering how to explain to his grandchildren.

I take solace in the fact that the outrage seems felt by both whites and blacks. Some white empathy may have dissipated with the violence; that same juror seemed to take considerable satisfaction in saying that what they were doing was much worse than what those cops had done. One black woman stood watching looters, tears rolling down her face, and said she couldn't understand how they could bring their children to steal. "I'm ashamed of my own people," she said.

I know that feeling. So why does it seem so impossible for her and me and millions like us to have a meeting of the minds until finally the met minds take precedence over the closed ones?

In 1968 the Kerner Commission released a report that talked of two Americas, one black, one white, separate and unequal. And I looked at my eight-year-old and thought that maybe in 2018, he would write the fiftieth-anniversary piece saying that nothing much had changed. I wondered if he would remember how he felt this last terrible week, or whether he would just be another brown-eyed child. I've tried to teach him that prejudice is intolerable, but watching the videotape he learned a different lesson. I wanted better for him. For all of them.

ERIN GO BRAWL

March 14, 1992

I never felt entirely at home at St. Patrick's Day parades. As constituted by the Ancient Order of Hibernians—emphasis on the Ancient—they reminded me until recently of two perceptions of the Irish: as silver-haired civil servants redolent of Old Spice, and as intoxicated teenagers throwing up into the hedges of Central Park.

Neither of those is me, and I am Irish and proud of it. But then, both of those stereotypes have their limits. A woman was grand marshal of the parade not long ago, and the ranks are now filled with black and Latino children who attend the city's parochial schools. The parade has changed.

But not enough.

Ethnic stereotypes are misshapen pearls, sometimes with a sandy grain of truth at their center. It is true that my forebears were the folks for whom the paddy wagon was named, because of the number of them taken away drunk and disorderly on long-ago Saturday nights. The words Tammany Hall speak for themselves. We are storytellers, accomplished mourners, devout Catholics.

And we are none of these. Because all of them are stereotypes.

And now we are stereotyped as antediluvian bigots, because the Ancient Order of Hibernians—still Ancient—decided to deny the Irish Lesbian and Gay Organization permission to march in the parade. First the organization was told there was no room, which is a familiar line to anyone who has read the Christmas story.

Then, after the mayor said that room could be made, the addition to the parade was judged "impractical," which is familiar to anyone who has dealt with a bureaucracy and is a fancy way of saying "we don't want to."

Finally, the gay group was told that its members could march if they melted into other groups and did not carry their banner, which is a familiar request to all who have ever been forced to deny what they are, closeted by the will of the majority.

Ethnic stereotypes are sometimes based on observed behavior, but they ignore complexity, change, and individuality. My earliest perception of my countrymen was of people shaped by blighted potatoes and empty stomachs, people who held fast to what they had and so sometimes had a closed fist. Like many immigrant groups, they found contempt and hatred everywhere, and so they drew together, in neighborhoods, churches, fraternal organizations.

Some characteristics of the Irish I know and love have always seemed to me contradictory. Hail fellows well met, without being met at all. The unknowable extroverts. It is no accident that some have taken to professions that give the illusion of being among the people while remaining essentially separate. Newspapermen, who are of events but outside them. Politicos, who always stand apart in the crowd. Priests.

Stereotypes, of course. If you see it differently, I understand.

But understand that the stereotypes about gay people grow not from small knowledge inflated but from ignorance writ large.

"No queers in the parade," people on Staten Island shouted at the mayor. These are the cries of those who don't know any gay people—or, more accurately, don't know they know any—and so create the bogeyman. Pederasts, drag queens, instead of the reality: the man at the next desk, the girl you went to high school with. Ordinary people who are gay. And Irish. And proud.

I can't imagine why those people want to march after what has happened. The A.O.H. has made a mess of this. When it barred gay people, there was the suspicion that it was reflecting the faith of its fathers, which considers homosexual acts sinful. But when it also barred a group of kids in wheelchairs—kids! in wheelchairs!—it appeared that it had forgotten that faith entirely. Hope those guys never get a chance to run Lourdes.

This is a parade that should belong to everyone. But they turned it into something that belongs to none of us, or at least none of us who have been stung by stereotype, none of us who were raised on the memory of the signs that said NO IRISH because all employers were sure the Irish were lazy and unreliable.

The members of the Ancient Order of Hibernians should remember those signs. They tried to hang a variation on Fifth Avenue this year. And in doing so they tarnished not the gay community but their own. Everything they've done stinks of stereotype, of the small-minded Irishman. For all of us who know that stereotypes exist to reduce understanding, not to enlarge it, I say they should be ashamed of themselves.

NO CLOSET
SPACE

May 27, 1992

It was twenty years ago next month that an elementary school teacher named Jeanne Manford made history. She walked down a street in New York City carrying the sort of poster paper her students sometimes used for projects, except that printed on it were these words: PARENTS of gays UNITE in SUPPORT for our CHILDREN

At her side during the Gay Pride march was her son, Morty, her golden boy, the one the teacher once told her would be a senator someday. When he was in high school he said he wanted to see a psychologist, and the psychologist called the Manfords in and told them that the golden boy was gay. But it never changed his mother's mind about his glow.

Morty's story, and his mother's, too, are contained in a new oral history of the gay struggle, *Making History,* by Eric Marcus. The cheering thing about the book is how far we have come since the days when newspaper editors felt free to use "homo" in headlines. The distressing thing is how far we have to go, not in the world alone, where homophobia remains one of the last acceptable bigotries, but in our homes, where our children learn that the world is composed exclusively of love and sex between men and women. Even when Mom and Dad have gay friends and raised consciousness, there is too often a silence that surrounds other ways of life and love. And silence begets distance.

Distance between parent and child is one of the saddest things discussed in *Making History:* the parents who try to commit their gay children to mental hospitals, the ones who erect a gravestone and send an obituary to the paper when they discover their daughter is a lesbian, or the ones who were told nothing because their children considered the truth untellable.

Greg Brock, a newspaperman, describes how he came out to his parents the day before he was to appear on the *Oprah Winfrey* show. Thirty-five years old and the man had never spoken to his mother and father of his central reality. "I was about to destroy my dad's life," he recalled.

Is this really what we want, to obsess about ear infections and reading readiness and then discover many years too late that we were either unaware or unaccepting of who our children were? To keen "What will I tell my friends?" when our kids try to talk about their lives?

In the same borough in which Morty Manford grew up and his mother taught, a Queens school board has rejected a curriculum that encourages respect for all families, including those headed by gay and lesbian parents. Consider that decision, not in terms of gay rights, but in terms of the children.

Given statistical estimates, the board is telling one out of ten kids that the life they will eventually lead is not part of the human program. Among their students are surely boys and girls who will discover they are gay and who, from their earliest years, will have learned that there is something wrong with them. Learned it from classmates, from teachers. Worst of all, from their own mothers and fathers.

Actually, it's probably the mothers and fathers who need that curriculum most. All parents should be aware that when they mock or curse gay people, they may be mocking or cursing their own child.

All parents should know that when they consider this subject unspeakable, they may be forever alienating their own child and causing enormous pain. Paulette Goodman, president of the Federation of Parents and Friends of Lesbians and Gays, likens it to her experience as a Jew in occupied Paris. "I know what it's like to be in the closet," she recalled. "I know all too well."

Jeanne Manford didn't want a closet. Her Morty was the same golden boy after she found out he was gay as he was before. She was with him at the Gay Pride march and with him in the gay rights movement.

And she was with him when he died a little more than a week ago of AIDS, almost twenty years to the day after she wrote her unconditional love on poster paper for all the world to see. She does not reproach herself. She loved and accepted her child the way he was. In a perfect world, this would be the definition of "parent" in the dictionary. The point is not what you'll tell your friends at the bridge table. It is what you'll tell yourself at the end.

WITH EXTREME
PREJUDICE

June 24, 1992

The story of Colonel Margarethe Cammermeyer had a certain déjà-vu-all-over-again quality. It might as easily have been the story of Sergeant Leonard Matlovich or Sergeant Miriam Ben Shalom or one of several other soldiers whose job histories included decorations, promotions, excellent evaluations.

For Colonel Cammermeyer, the honors included a Bronze Star for her work as a nurse in Vietnam and recognition as the Veterans Administration Nurse of the Year. None of it made any difference when she was dismissed from the Washington State National Guard, one of thousands of Americans whose exemplary service has paled beside the military's determination to boot gay soldiers.

Many in the service will tell you that this is a difficult issue, as is the question of women in combat and other adjustments the Army, Navy, Air Force, and Marines have been asked to make to the twentieth century.

It is not difficult at all. It comes down to this: Will we continue to support one of America's largest and best-known institutions as it, not simply by custom but by regulation, engages in the rankest forms of discrimination?

The question is particularly apt as the Navy finds itself embroiled in a sickening sexual-harassment scandal. If you were wondering where your defense dollars go, almost $200,000 of them were spent to fly naval aviators to a military frat party in Las Vegas last year at which Navy women were passed down a gauntlet of their male colleagues, grabbed and mauled in a form of hand-to-hand combat not taught in basic training. An aide to an admiral had to resort to biting one flyboy who pushed his hand inside her bra during this group grope, which apparently had become something of a Navy tradition.

There is wailing and gnashing of teeth about this by the brass, a search for blame and underlying cause. It seems never to have occurred to them that if you treat women like second-class citizens by denying them promotion to combat positions, your male personnel will get the idea that they can treat them like second-class citizens in other ways, too. And that if you make homosexuality the modern equivalent of godless Communism, then hetero conduct in even its most abusive forms may seem sanctioned, even blessed.

The Vegas incident renders almost comical the fear of allowing gay people into the military. Same-sex propositions seem sedate compared with being pushed down a long hallway of guys with nuclear hands and Cro-Magnon mores.

But that is not the underlying cause of this ban. It is the perceived comfort level of straight male soldiers. The term of art is "cohesiveness," what we civilians might call male bonding. In other words, they may have to fight or serve beside those with whom they lack proper kinship.

This is the argument once used to keep black soldiers in segregated units, a bit of military history that seems unthinkable today. And it has also been used to oppose allowing women in combat. (There's also the argument of the pedestal, the idea that male soldiers will spend all their time protecting their female counter-parts. I imagine the admiral's aide would have some choice words about that.) It's funny to read about a new Navy training program that, for the first time in history, features sexually integrated boot camp. After all the arguments about fatal distractions, they've discovered that putting men and women together actually improves training and fosters the much-vaunted cohesion. "It's more cooperative and there's more teamwork," said one instructor. Armed forces, meet real life.

According to the General Accounting Office, the prohibition on gay people in the military costs us at least $27 million a year, given the fact that a thousand men and women are dismissed and replaced. That's an absurd waste of time and money.

But more important is the fact that the military continues to piously justify retaining regulations that are no more than codified prejudice. Officials sometimes say this is the will of the people; if they are keeping track, seven in ten think women should be permitted to occupy combat positions and 50 percent see no reason to keep gay people out of the military.

Instead of stooping to a comfort level of ignorance, the military should reflect the simple notion of performance as the gauge of job fitness. Besides, maybe their notion of comfort level is all wrong. Maybe there are no homophobes in foxholes.

EVAN'S TWO MOMS

February 5, 1992

Evan has two moms. This is no big thing. Evan has always had two moms—in his school file, on his emergency forms, with his friends. "Ooooh, Evan, you're lucky," they sometimes say. "You have two moms." It sounds like a sitcom, but until last week it was emotional truth without legal bulwark. That was when a judge in New York approved the adoption of a six-year-old boy by his biological mother's lesbian partner. Evan. Evan's mom. Evan's other mom. A kid, a psychologist, a pediatrician. A family.

The matter of Evan's two moms is one in a series of events over the last year that lead to certain conclusions. A Minnesota appeals court granted guardianship of a woman left a quadriplegic in a car accident to her lesbian lover, the culmination of a seven-year battle in which the injured woman's parents did everything possible to negate the partnership between the two. A lawyer in Georgia had her job offer withdrawn after the state attorney general found out that she and her lesbian lover were planning a marriage ceremony; she's brought suit. The computer company Lotus announced that the gay partners of employees would be eligible for the same benefits as spouses.

Add to these public events the private struggles, the couples who go from lawyer to lawyer to approximate legal protections their straight counterparts take for granted, the AIDS survivors who find themselves shut out of their partners' dying days by biological family members and shut out of their apartments by leases with a single name on the dotted line, and one solution is obvious.

Gay marriage is a radical notion for straight people and a conservative notion for gay ones. After years of being sledgehammered by society, some gay men and lesbian women are deeply suspicious of participating in an institution that seems to have "straight world" written all over it.

But the rads of twenty years ago, straight and gay alike, have other things on their minds today. Family is one, and the linchpin of family has commonly been a loving commitment between two adults. When same-sex couples set out to make that commitment, they discover that they are at a disadvantage: No joint tax returns. No health insurance coverage for an uninsured partner. No survivor's benefits from Social Security. None of the automatic rights, privileges, and responsibilities society attaches to a marriage contract. In Madison, Wisconsin, a couple who applied at the Y with their kids for a family membership were turned down because both were women. It's one of those small things that can make you feel small.

Some took marriage statutes that refer to "two persons" at their word and applied for a license. The results were court decisions that quoted the Bible and embraced circular argument: marriage is by definition the union of a man and a woman because that is how we've defined it.

No religion should be forced to marry anyone in violation of its tenets, although ironically it is now only in religious ceremonies that gay people can marry, performed by clergy who find the blessing of two who love each other no sin. But there is no secular reason that we should take a patchwork approach of corporate, governmental, and legal steps to guarantee what can be done simply, economically, conclusively, and inclusively with the words "I do."

"Fran and I chose to get married for the same reasons that any two people do," said the lawyer who was fired in Georgia. "We fell in love; we wanted to spend our lives together." Pretty simple.

Consider the case of *Loving* v. *Virginia*, aptly named. At the time, sixteen states had laws that barred interracial marriage, relying on natural law, that amorphous grab bag for justifying prejudice. Sounding a little like God throwing Adam and Eve out of paradise, the trial judge suspended the one-year sentence of Richard Loving, who was white, and his wife, Mildred, who was black, provided they got out of the state of Virginia.

In 1967 the Supreme Court found such laws to be unconstitutional. Only twenty-five years ago and it was a crime for a black woman to marry a white man. Perhaps twenty-five years from now we will find it just as incredible that two people of the same sex were not entitled to legally commit themselves to each other. Love and commitment are rare enough; it seems absurd to thwart them in any guise.

MOVING THE FURNITURE AROUND

December 2, 1990

The man who wears an Army blanket and holds out a cardboard coffee cup in the Christopher Street subway station has a method to what some might call his madness. When he is told to leave the landing there, he goes two blocks down to the station from which trains run beneath the Hudson River to New Jersey. If that station is inhospitable, short on commuters or long on cops, he walks east to the West Fourth Street subway station. And he goes back to Christopher Street if there are problems at West Fourth.

The subway has always been a good place to collect money. It is not uncommon to sit on a train and have the narrow tube filled with fund-raisers' speechifying: "Good afternoon, ladies and gentleman. I represent the Sons of the Lord community outreach program in Brooklyn!" It is not unheard of to sit on a train and find your life on the line: "Give me your money or I'll cut you bad." The definition of a captive audience is a dozen people on an express train between stations.

But the New York City Transit Authority has banned begging

THINKING OUT LOUD / 37

on the subway, and the Supreme Court last week let stand that ban. The legal pavane included pages of discussion of whether begging is speech or begging is behavior. For my acquaintance in the Christopher Street station, begging is a container of coffee, a buttered roll, and a bottle of bad wine.

Once again, we've wasted time and money by dealing with the homeless backward. Too much energy has gone into deciding where we do not want them to be, and making sure that they would not be there. Benches were outfitted with dividers so that no one could lie down. Police were taught to turn people out of public buildings. And the Transit Authority rousted them off trains. The exercise is reminiscent of moving furniture in a small apartment; you can put the couch in a number of places, but you cannot make it unobtrusive. The secret is to find a place where the couch fits.

There is no doubt that some of the homeless belong in psychiatric hospitals, but the number is probably much smaller than we believe. Mary Scullion, who runs two communal homes for women in Philadelphia, took a census five years ago of habitual street dwellers in Center City, identified by name and location 115 who appeared to be mentally ill, and set out to see if they were salvageable. Today, only five of them are in long-term psychiatric care. Eight are still on the streets. The rest are living in supervised residences or with their families.

Four years ago a woman named Ellen Baxter opened a single-room-occupancy building in upper Manhattan for homeless men and women. Today she is preparing to open her fifth building, a $4 million city-financed renovation that contains seventy-five studio apartments for individuals and seven two-bedroom apartments for families. None of the people in her buildings need to be in institutions, but few of them are ready to live without the assistance of the staff Columbia University provides, to help with their medical problems and their addictions, to negotiate the social service maze and what Ms. Baxter calls "the paperwork of poverty."

We can do much more of this, or we can continue to waste time and money moving these people around like so much furniture. One of the craziest ladies on the streets of Center City, a woman considered totally lost to normal life, lives in a group residence and works full time now, and Mary Scullion says that since that woman has been getting enough food and sleep and medical attention it's amazing, the resemblance she bears to you or me.

Discussions about the homeless always remind me of a woman who told me that she was damned if her tax dollars were going to pay for birth control for the poor. Come to think of it, she said, she didn't want her tax dollars paying for any social welfare programs. I wanted to say to her: If you don't pay for birth control, you'll have to pay for schools. If you don't pay for schools, you're going to pay for welfare. And if you don't pay for any of those things, you're going to spend a small fortune on prisons.

The question is not whether we will pay. It is what we want to pay for, and what works. The negative approach, the deciding where we want people not to be, has been a deplorable failure. There are those who believe the homeless are either criminal or crazy, that one way or another they should be locked up. It's worth remembering that it costs far more to lock someone up than to give them, as Ms. Scullion and Ms. Baxter have, a key of their own.

ROOM AT THE INN

December 11, 1991

Ten years ago Harold Brown decided to do something that he
had never done before but that he believed his Catholic faith
required him to do. He began to help house the homeless. He
and his wife, Virginia, and a group of volunteers from Sacred
Heart Church in Queens set up a small shelter in the basement
of the church in response to a call to action from the mayor, the
cardinal, and the Partnership for the Homeless.

For a decade they have provided a bed each night, as well as
breakfast, a bag lunch, a hot dinner, a change of underclothes,
and, after the plumber hooked up extra waterlines, a shower and
the use of a washer and dryer. The city housed almost seventy-five
hundred people in shelters the other night; Sacred Heart housed
ten. Alleluia and pass the excuses. This is an answer to people
who have said they'd like to help the homeless but don't know
how.

This is an answer to all those people who find the holidays a
fearsome round of eggnog and revolving charges. It doesn't have

to be that way. Even now there are friends preparing polite ecstasies for gifts they neither want nor need. Even now there are people penciling your party into their datebooks and quietly wishing they could spend the day at home.

The important thing to remember about Christmas is not closing time at Macy's but the story of a pregnant woman and her husband who looked for a bed for what some still think was the most transformative event in history and were told to get lost. The irony of the fact that there is no room at the inn for millions in this country is potent at this time.

Ten years ago this month the Partnership for the Homeless began the church/synagogue network with a simple premise: that with thousands of institutions in New York built on charity and compassion, surely there must be some willing to provide a bed for the night. Tonight there will be something like 1,365 homeless people sleeping in 126 churches and synagogues. At a time when homeless men and women are being rousted from public buildings, subway stations, and assorted doorways, apparently in the belief that a moving target is less offensive to community comfort levels, that is no small thing.

These small shelters, all with fewer than twenty beds, are scattered throughout the city. Their success gives the lie to dire predictions surrounding the city's plan to build small shelters in residential areas, predictions ranging from plummeting property values to soaring crime. Mr. Brown says he was "scared to death" of opposition when the parishioners opened their little place in the community of Glendale, which is where Archie Bunker was said to have had his home. Last Sunday Mr. Brown took up a collection to pay for food for shelter guests. At the end of the day there was $1,100 in the baskets. Last month he called for more volunteers. Fifty people put their names on the list.

Surely there are more churches and synagogues out there that could do this. Surely a shelter in the basement would do more to teach the values that are supposed to inform the holidays than a hundred sermons.

Surely there is more connection with Christmas in setting up cots and serving stew than in the frenetic round of the season, which is habitually cited as exhausting and rarely as satisfying. Parents have railed against shelters near schools, but no one has made any connection between the crazed consumerism of our kids and their elders' cold unconcern toward others. Maybe the homeless are not the only ones who need to spend time in these places to thaw out.

We question the efficiency of government, and with good cause. We say that something permanent needs to be done, and that is true. And if we agree that government has done a rotten job reducing the quotient of human misery, Mr. Brown has an alternative: Do it yourself.

"I work in midtown," says Mr. Brown, who is a vice president in futures and options at Dean Witter, "and I saw these poor souls on the subway grates. We're just trying to do what Christ asked us to do." That is, to do good. Boy, does that seem distant from the white noise of modern life. "If I am for myself alone, what good am I?" said the Jewish sage Hillel two thousand years ago, around the time that his coreligionists Mary and Joseph found themselves homeless in Bethlehem. And if the time to act is not now, when will it be?

NO PLACE·LIKE HOME

May 20, 1992

Homeless is like the government wanting you locked up
And the people in America do not like you.
They look at you and say Beast!
I wish the people would help the homeless
And stop their talking.

—FRANK S. RICE,
the *Rio Times*

The building is beautiful, white and beige and oak, the colors of yuppies. The rehab of the Rio came in seven-hundred-thousand dollars under budget, two months ahead of schedule. The tenants say they will not mess it up, no, no, no. "When you don't have a place and you get a good place, the last thing you want to do is lose it," said one man who slept in shelters for seven years—seven years during which you might have gotten married, or lost a loved one, or struck it rich, but all this guy did was live on the streets.

Mayor David Dinkins has announced that he will study parts of the study he commissioned from a commission on the homeless, the newest in a long line of studies.

One study, done in 1981, was called "Private Lives, Public Spaces." It was researched by Ellen Baxter, who now runs the nonprofit company that has brought us the Rio and four other buildings that provide permanent housing for the homeless in Washington Heights.

Another study, done in 1987, was called "A Shelter Is Not a Home" and was produced by the Manhattan Borough president, David Dinkins, who now runs the city of New York. At the time, the Koch administration said it would study Mr. Dinkins's study, which must have taught Mr. Dinkins something.

Robert Hayes, one of the founding fathers of the movement to help the homeless, once told me there were three answers to the problem: housing, housing, housing. It was an overly simplistic answer, and it was essentially correct.

Despite our obsessions with pathology and addiction, Ms. Baxter has renovated one apartment building after another and filled them with people. At the Rio, what was once a burnt-out eyesore is now, with its curving façade and bright lobby, the handsomest building on the block; what were once armory transients with dirt etched in the creases of hands and face are now tenants. The building needed people; the people needed a home. The city provided the rehab money; Columbia University provides social service support.

Some of the tenants need to spend time in drug treatment and some go to Alcoholics Anonymous and some of them lapse into pretty pronounced fugue states from time to time. So what? How would you behave if you'd lived on the streets for seven years? What is better: To leave them out there while we lament the emptying of the mental hospitals and the demise of jobs? Or to provide a roof over their heads and then get them psychiatric care and job training?

What is better: To spend nearly $20,000 each year to have

them sleep on cots at night and wander the streets by day? Or to make a onetime investment of $38,000 a unit, as they did in the single rooms with kitchens and baths in the Rio, for permanent homes for people who will pay rent from their future wages or from entitlement benefits?

Years ago I became cynical enough to envision a game plan in which politicians, tussling over government stuff like demonstration projects and agency jurisdiction and commission studies, ignored this problem until it went away.

And, in a sense, it has. We have become so accustomed to people sleeping on sidewalks and in subway stations that recumbent bodies have become small landmarks in our neighborhoods. Mary Brosnahan, executive director of the Coalition for the Homeless, says she was stunned, talking to students, at their assumption that people always had and always would be living on the streets. My children call by pet names—"the man with the cup," "the lady with the falling-down pants"—the homeless people around their school.

And when a problem becomes that rooted in our everyday perceptions, it is understood to be without solution. Nonprofit groups like the one that renovated the Rio prove that this is not so. The cots in the armory are poison; drug programs and job training are icing. A place to shut the door, to sleep without one eye open, to be warm, to be safe—that's the cake. There's no place like home. You didn't need a study to figure that out, did you?

SOMALIA'S PLAGUES

September 6, 1992

The two children are the last survivors of their family, but not, it appears, for long. In news footage they sit naked on the ground, their spindly arms wrapped around each other, the inevitability of their imminent death in their sunken eyes. In their homeland, rent by internal power struggles, there is no food, and so they starve while worlds away the politicians puzzle over what to do.

But these children are not in Bosnia, now the center of world attention. They are in Somalia, an African country living through—and dying of—a lethal combination of clan warfare, drought, and famine that has wrought what one U.S. official called the worst humanitarian crisis in the world right now.

Millions of people in Somalia are in danger of starving to death in the months to come. Hundreds will die today. Although the International Red Cross has mounted the largest relief effort in its history, it is too dangerous to take food to some areas, and supplies are often stolen by gunmen and sold by profiteers. Relief kitchens have graveyards flanking them, so that those who die on food lines may be buried while the line moves on.

Eurocentrism was a kind of catchword not long ago amid the scornful discussion of multicultural curricula in the public schools. Were we going to throw out Shakespeare, cease to teach the Magna Carta, minimize the role of Napoleon in world affairs?

But the truth is that we are a deeply Eurocentric nation, and for obvious reasons. Many of us have Euroroots, and from the beginning we have sought Euroalliances. When we hear of Serbian-run concentration camps we relate them, with renewed outrage, to the atrocities of Nazi Germany. When Americans see Bosnian orphans crying in the windows of buses, offers pour in to adopt them.

Bosnia, with all its horrors, is at the center of public and political dialogue, and Somalia, with all its horrors, is a peripheral discussion. "It's racism," says Jack Healey, executive director of Amnesty International.

And a peculiar sort of myopic ignorance. Civil war and unconscionable internment in Bosnia seem man-made evils, subject to man-made solutions. But Africa is a mystery to our Eurocentric nation, even to many African-Americans. Its troubles seem like Old Testament plagues, irresolvable and inevitable.

There is nothing inevitable about the corpses littering the landscape of Somalia. There are no easy solutions for a nation of nomads who have been prevented from planting crops by the ravages of civil war, a country that has almost no government aside from village elders in dying towns.

There are no easy solutions in the former Yugoslavia, either, where factional hatreds are a tangled web stretching back centuries. But there is now sharply focused attention by the international community on what should be done and who should do it. Somalia deserves that same intense attention, from George Bush, Bill Clinton, the American people, and our allies abroad.

The United Nations has agreed to airlift food into the interior, but that is neither an adequate nor a long-term solution. Senator

Nancy Kassebaum, who sits on the Senate subcommittee on African affairs, supports the use of an international force of soldiers to make sure food shipments get to the people. But she also says the United States must have a continuing commitment to development in African nations instead of a crisis-management approach.

Just a year ago some of us, unpersuaded by the high moral principles involved in giving our all for cheap oil, were saying that America could no longer afford to police the world. With the president's Gulf-war bluster about liberation, we lost sight of the best reason to involve ourselves in foreign affairs—because it is sometimes obviously the moral thing to do.

The new secretary general of the United Nations, Boutros Boutros-Ghali, an Egyptian who is the first leader of the U.N. from the continent of Africa, has referred to the Bosnian conflict as the "rich man's war." He means it is a white man's war, a Eurowar, in its combatants, its victims, and its international interest. That makes aid no less necessary. Just as the color of its children must make no difference in our help for Somalia. Surely our attention span can encompass two mortal crises at once. Surely our empathy can transcend race.

SEEKING A SENSE OF CONTROL

December 10, 1990

Many years ago I took a stroll around the block with the mother of a friend. As we walked she made sudden noises, like shots from a gun. But when I listened carefully it seemed that the sounds were orphaned bits of words, as though her conversation were a tape and most of it had been erased, leaving only stray fricatives and glottal stops. Perhaps the sounds were the remaining shreds of her personality, which had been taken into some dark place by a then little-known ailment called Alzheimer's disease.

This may have been the sort of life Janet Adkins feared when she lay in a Volkswagen van and pressed the button that released lethal drugs into her body. Mrs. Adkins's doctor believed she had years to go before her self disappeared into the degenerative swamp of Alzheimer's. But anyone who has ever encountered the disease knows its Catch-22; by the time you might want to die, you're too far gone to do anything about it. Mrs. Adkins, a former English teacher, looked into the future and committed suicide.

If she had done so alone, her story would be a small one. But she went to Jack Kevorkian, a euthanasia entrepreneur who constructed a suicide machine at home. Mrs. Adkins used it to go quietly into that good night. And Dr. Kevorkian was charged with first-degree murder.

This is the sort of case prosecutors characterize as "sending a message," as though we were unruly schoolchildren waiting to throw rocks through the windows of the law. Mrs. Adkins could have accomplished what she sought with a handgun or a tall building. But she went to Dr. Kevorkian because she wanted a gentle death, the kind we offer now even for some of those we execute.

There is a message in this case, but it is not the one prosecutors send. It illustrates how desperate we have become to retain some modicum of control in the face not only of horrible illness but of medical protocols that lengthen degeneration and dying. There are probably few Americans who, like Mrs. Adkins, want to end their lives while they are still unmarred by illness. And only one country, the Netherlands, permits physician-assisted suicide. But there are thousands of people who find that after the chemotherapy and the surgeries and the progression of disease they have become a macabre mockery of their former selves, keeping their lives but losing their dignity.

Once a friend told me that her mother, who was suffering from ovarian cancer, had a superb oncologist. He was kind and considerate and explained all procedures thoroughly. But she blurted out what was his great virtue: "He told me how many of my mother's painkillers constituted a lethal dose."

There are doctors like that, who go quietly about the business of tempering science with mercy. A pneumonia goes untreated; a new course of chemo is not tried. The American Hospital Association says 70 percent of the deaths that occur in this country include some negotiated agreement not to use life-prolonging technology.

The case of Nancy Cruzan may end soon, although her parents

believe her life ended years ago. The State of Missouri, after fighting all the way to the Supreme Court, has withdrawn its opposition to having the thirty-two-year-old woman's feeding tube removed. The cases of Nancy Cruzan, who has been in a persistent vegetative state for seven years, and Janet Adkins, who discussed her planned suicide with her family, are worlds apart. And yet both the Cruzan family and Mrs. Adkins yearned for the same thing: a sense of control.

Hard cases make bad law, my lawyer says, and this is one. Dr. Kevorkian, an assisted-suicide zealot who has been a guest on *Donahue,* had a vested interest in Mrs. Adkin's decision to end her life. But hard cases sometimes illuminate hard issues. The medical profession must continue to find ways to balance its capabilities and their human costs. The people must demand laws that allow them to participate in that balancing, laws that embody the facts of their lives.

The question of how and when we die, in an age of respirators and antibiotics and feed tubes, has become one of the great "who decides?" issues of modern time. When Nancy Cruzan's case was being heard, people with medical war stories said: "Wheel her into the courtroom. Then they'll understand." Perhaps that is what Janet Adkins did: placed the evidence before the judge she believed knew best, saw herself incontinent, incompetent, incapable of knowing the difference between *Tom and Jerry* and *War and Peace.* And then pronounced sentence.

A TIME TO
DIE

June 3, 1990

When she visits her husband in the nursing home, she apologizes
to him. Ann is a nurse, and her husband was a carpenter, and
when they came home from work in the old days, before the accident, she would tell him about the people on machines, the respirators, and the feeding tubes. And he would say, "If that ever
happens to me, I want you to shoot me."

As his eyes stare out into some middle distance from his hospital bed, his feeding tube a small stigma in his side, she tells him
she is sorry she cannot do what he asked.

The American Academy of Neurology defines a persistent vegetative state thus: "A form of eyes-open permanent unconscious-
ness in which the patient has periods of wakefulness and
physiologic sleep/wake cycles, but at no time is the patient aware
of himself or his environment." There may be as many as ten
thousand people in this condition in the United States. Ann's
husband has been one of them since the night before Thanksgiving in 1986, when his car didn't make the curve.

He is thirty.

She is twenty-nine.

She feels as if her husband died three years ago and she's waiting for the funeral. Three times she has asked to have the feeding tube removed. The hospital said no. The nursing home said no.

The lawyer said, "Wait for *Cruzan*."

There are many stories like this one in America, but the one we know best now is the story of thirty-two-year-old Nancy Cruzan. She once told a friend she would never want to be kept alive as a vegetable. Her parents have spent eight years arguing that that is important, arguing that she would not want to continue life in a persistent vegetative state, arguing that her feeding tube should be removed. Any day now the Supreme Court will decide whether this can be done, whether there is a constitutional right to discontinue unwanted life-sustaining treatment.

Right now there is a patchwork of state regulation and case law on this matter. In some places you can remove a respirator but not a feeding tube. In some places you can remove a feeding tube if a patient left written instructions, but not if he simply said he wouldn't want one.

In most places people who are spending their lives staring at the contorted, withered shell of someone they love dearly must go to court to do what they think best. Many of them never make it. There are the legal costs. A retainer of $10,000 is not exorbitant, given the amount of time spent on a case like this, but for most Americans, it might as well be $10 million.

And there is the holier-than-thou factor. One family in Oregon, whose son was drowned at age six and died at age nineteen, never went to court to have his feeding tube removed because, his mother said, they didn't want problems with right-to-life zealots. In New York State, a bill that would allow people to designate someone to make medical decisions if they were incapacitated has been kicking around the Legislature for a year, supported by groups ranging from the Lutherans to the Gay

Men's Health Crisis Center. The state Right to Life Committee has been vehement in its opposition. That sort of reaction is why Ann's last name does not appear here. She is afraid of the right-to-life types, of the hate mail and the publicity they bring. "Yes, I am," she says.

She doesn't go to see her husband much. Most of the time she believes she is looking at a shell. Sometimes she thinks there is a spark inside. I don't know which is worse: a body being kept alive while no one is home or a bit of a man trapped, like a fly in a bottle, unable to talk, to see, to touch—just like a ghost.

The Supreme Court may not see fit to provide constitutional salvation for these people. But just as the *Webster* decision has galvanized those who want abortion to remain legal, perhaps *Cruzan* will remind us that we must demand reasonable regulations to help people whose husbands, fathers, daughters have become the living dead. Someday we could be beside the bed, or in it.

There must be some reasonable way to allow someone to speak for us when we cannot speak for ourselves, some reasonable way to make the distinction between real life and the mirage modern medicine can create. A way that does not include years of court appearances and bedside vigils.

He asked her to shoot him.

I'm betting that if you stopped ten people on the street and asked them who should make this decision for that man, they would say his wife should.

"If he could talk," Ann said, "he'd be really angry at me for not doing what he asked."

JUSTICE
AND MERCY

July 29, 1990

Perhaps there comes a moment in the life of every woman when she yearns to telephone an 84-year-old man she has never met and ask, "How could you do this to me?"

For me, that moment came last week.

I am taking the resignation of Justice William Brennan personally. I have read all of some of his opinions, and bits of others, and I know where he dissented and where he pulled together a tenuous majority. And I keep remembering the speech in *The Merchant of Venice* about mercy tempering justice.

Over the years I have come to believe that as a member of that mysterious body the Supreme Court he was someone who was in my corner, who touched my life from within one of those pale official tombs that line the streets of Washington. "The lightning rod for individual rights and individual freedom," Barbara Jordan called him on television—the man who once referred to the treatment of women as "'romantic paternalism' which, in practi-

THINKING OUT LOUD / 55

cal effect, put women not on a pedestal, but in a cage." That's how I thought of him the morning after he called it quits. Not too shabby for an ordinary guy appointed by Ike.

He was a kinder, gentler justice. One reason why that well-wrought phrase has become so potent is that it is so patently false. We have the sour disposition of a country with diminished expectations, a country whose people have been living through a depression both economic and spiritual.

It is a depression our government refuses to acknowledge, so the American people live with a sinking feeling that their sinking standard of living is a failure of the individual. "I really don't feel as if politicians have any connection to me personally," a college student told me. Our elections are as big, bright, and empty as balloons.

Only one branch of our tripartite system is not governed by the ballot box, and that is the judiciary. No commercials with the flag rippling in the breeze, no slogans ("Blackmun—because it's your body"), no limits on term of office. Nine private people spend their lives defining our own through cases. Behind those cases there are always human beings, who want to be spared loyalty oaths and censorship, who want to buy birth-control devices, and who want to be admitted to good colleges. Justice Brennan seemed to pick the people out of the fact patterns, and to respond to their problems and their pain. Justice and mercy. Maybe that was not his job, but I'm glad he did it.

America is a country that seems forever to be either toddler or teenager, at those two stages of human development character-ized by conflict between autonomy and security. While some interpret this to mean we want neither to use the potty nor have a curfew, it's a tension that is one of our great strengths. Justice Brennan stressed both sides, the right to have government leave us alone in some cases and be our defender in others. The rights of the accused. Free speech, however objectionable. Affirmative action. The right to die, to do what we please in our bedrooms, to be protected from sex discrimination. The discussion of his retirement has centered on a single right, the right to a legal abortion, and that is sad because his vision is larger than that.

His detractors saw it as too large, a liberal agenda that made the Court into a legislator of public policy, not an interpreter of the Constitution. Judge Robert Bork, whose nomination to the High Court was rejected by the Senate and who is still smarting from the rebuff, calls Justice Brennan "imperialistic." Judge Bork is a fan of the framers, those increasingly popular guys who actually made up the Constitution, and whose intent has become a matter of great moment to some jurists. We have judges who talk about the framers as though they played squash with them regularly. It reminds you of the proprietary, slightly arrogant way in which born-again Christians talk about God. They know Him; you don't.

The only thing I know about the framers is that they were general kinds of guys. They didn't go on about the right to put fences around your farmland, or the right to pull your children out of school if the teacher taught sedition. They used broad terms. Life. Property. Liberty. They designed a document that wouldn't go out of fashion. Written by men whose wives couldn't vote and whose country permitted slavery, it has transcended their time.

Justice Brennan made it transcendent. His work is full of empathy, and that is an uncommon thing, not only in a judge but in our society. We rarely take government personally, and so I was surprised to feel personally disfranchised by his loss. I prize what Justice Louis Brandeis called "the right to be let alone." I'm an individual. One of the best friends an individual ever had has left the arena, and we will all miss him, whether we know it yet or not.

PARENTAL RITES

September 25, 1991

Adolescence is a tough time for parent and child alike. It is a time between: between childhood and maturity, between parental protection and personal responsibility, between life stage-managed by grown-ups and life privately held. Past thirteen, shy of twenty, our children seem to fire off from time to time like a barrel full of Roman candles. Prom pictures show them the way we want them, curled and clean.

A week ago, in his diocesan newspaper column, Cardinal O'Connor wrote of a call from a New York law firm offering to represent Catholic parents of public school students "if condoms are forced on such a youngster without parental consent." It's the verb that is the red flag in that sentence. The plan to make condoms available in New York City high schools has nothing to do with force. The scenario of the principal at the school door pressing prophylactics for extra credit on unwilling fourteen-year-old virgins is useful for those who are opposed to this project. But it is a fraud.

Teenagers who feel they need condoms will go to a specially designated room and receive them from a specially trained school staff member. Some will do this because they've been told condoms can protect against the AIDS virus. Some will do it because they've heard condoms can protect against sexually transmitted diseases. All will be assuming a degree of responsibility unusual in a person of seventeen. Chastity may be preferable, but if not adhered to, responsibility is critical, even lifesaving.

The idea of force in such a program is a sop for indignant parents. If we imagine teenagers being forced into condom use and, by extension, sex, we don't have to think of them as sexual beings choosing, despite our own moral imperatives, to be sexually active. If we imagine force, we don't have to wonder what role we parents have played; we can simply blame the schools, the liberal power structure, the social radicals.

At a Board of Education meeting earlier this month, the representative from Staten Island, Michael Petrides, announced, "There is no way in this city and in these United States that someone is going to tell my son he can have a condom when I say he can't." News flash, Mr. Petrides: Any drugstore clerk in America can do just that if your son has the money.

Other objections to the condom program are just as redolent of the seductive idea that we have absolute control over our kids, just as blind to what some teenagers need to stay healthy and obsessed with what some parents need to feel self-satisfied. If we are confident that they are chaste, there is nothing to worry about, despite the suggestion that condoms in the schools are the 1990's equivalent of Spanish Fly.

If we are not confident, there is plenty to worry about, the least of it condoms; there are diseases that can cause sterility and one that will even cause death. We have many years to try to shape small and malleable people into big ones who share the values we hold most dear. Sometimes we manage to do it. And sometimes we do not. To jeopardize their health because they have not turned out exactly as we planned is an extraordinarily selfish thing to do, reminiscent of a variation on that old vaudeville turn: Enough about me. Let's talk about you. How do you make me feel about myself?

The Board of Education has made it possible for some parents to continue to fool themselves. Those who don't want to know any more about their kids' sex life than they absolutely must will know that their sons and daughters are receiving education, counseling, even condoms at school. And those who want to believe that their kids don't have a sex life can blame the condom program if they find out differently.

The prom-picture kids exist for one reason only: to make parents feel good about themselves. And that is all well and good, I suppose, until the first time you see a girl with secondary syphilis in a hospital bed, or meet a teenager who has contracted AIDS from a sex partner. You look back on plagues of the past and you see how people hundreds of years ago dealt with them, see their quirks and foibles. Maybe someday it will seem quaint that, during a time of plague, some of the parents of the 1990s wanted to deny their children protection so that they could safeguard their own self-image. Or maybe we'll just seem like a bunch of lunatics.

BELIEVE IN
MAGIC

November 11, 1991

The last time we heard so much about a smile was when those ridiculous buttons surfaced a decade ago, the ones with the happy face and the legend "Have a nice day." Those were phony; Magic Johnson's smile is real, a grin that says feelgood as surely as the rest of him says basketball.

Some basketball players, because of their height and a certain hauteur, seem to demand genuflection. Magic Johnson always looks to me like a guy you should hug. That was especially true when he told the world he was infected with the AIDS virus, said he was going to become a national spokesman and flashed the grin nonetheless. What a man.

This is what AIDS looks like—good people, lovable people, people you want to hug. Are we finally ready to face that truth? Are we finally ready to behave properly instead of continuing to be infected by the horrible virus of bigotry and blindness that has accompanied this epidemic?

This is what AIDS looks like—good people who get sick.

Artists, actors, soldiers, sailors, writers, editors, politicians, priests. The same issue of *The New York Times* that carried the astounding story of Magic Johnson's announcement carried the deaths of four men with AIDS: an educational testing expert, an actor, a former dancer and choreographer, and a partner in a law firm. "Loving nature," said one death notice. "Generosity of spirit," said another. Beloved by family and friends.

In the ten years since five gay men with pneumonia became a million people who are HIV-positive, this illness has brought out the worst in America. We obsess about "life-style" in the midst of a pyramid scheme of mortality, an infectious disease spreading exponentially.

Over the last year, we have witnessed the canonization of one AIDS patient, a twenty-three-year-old woman named Kimberly Bergalis who says that she "didn't do anything wrong." This is code, and so is her elevation to national symbol. Kimberly Bergalis is a lovely white woman with no sexual history who contracted AIDS from her dentist. She is what some people like to call an "innocent victim."

With that single adjective we condemn those who get AIDS from sex and those who get it from dirty needles as guilty and ultimately unworthy of our help and sympathy. We imply that gay men deserve what they get and people who shoot up might as well be dead. It's a little like being sympathetic to the health-conscious jogger who dies of a heart attack during a stint on the Stairmaster but telling the widow of the couch potato, "Well, if he hadn't eaten all those hot dogs, this wouldn't have happened."

It's not how you get it; it's how you spread it. And we know how that happens and what to do about it. Education. Conversation. Prevention. I don't want to hear any more about how condoms shouldn't be advertised on television and in the newspapers. I don't want to hear any more about the impropriety of clean-needle exchanges or the immorality of AIDS education in the schools.

On Thursday night our eight-year-old asked about safe sex after he heard those words from Magic Johnson's mouth. And I was amazed at how simply and straightforwardly I was able to discuss it. Because I don't want to hear any more about good people who aren't going to live until their fortieth birthday, about wasted talent and missed chances and children who die long before their fathers and mothers do. I'm far less concerned about my kids' life-styles than I am about their lives.

How are all those parents who denigrate "queers" and "junkies" going to explain this one? How are all those pious people who like to talk about "innocent victims" going to deal with the lovable basketball star, the all-time sports hero, who stressed safe sex when he told the world he was HIV-positive? Will this finally make them say to their kids, "It could happen to you," finally make them stop relying solely on chastity and start dealing with reality?

"Marc will be greatly missed," said one of the death notices. Who cares where it began; this is where it ended, in small black letters on the obituary page. One good person after another, infected, then sick, and finally dying. Magic Johnson, with that engaging personality, that athletic legerdemain, that grin—this is what AIDS looks like. Why can't we learn to deal with our national tragedy with as much dignity and determination as this good man brings to his personal one?

FOUL PLAY

October 4, 1990

I've covered politics and I've covered crime, and I've liked doing them both. But one thing I understood about those assignments: sometimes you found yourself hanging around with a questionable class of people.

I've never covered sports, but I hear the same is true.

Lisa Olson covers sports for *The Boston Herald*. No matter what people think about getting free tickets and meeting celebrities, being a sports reporter is hard work. And the last thing you need, along with deadline pressure and road trips and working weekends for your foreseeable future life, is to have a clutch of football players position their genitals close to your face and make lewd suggestions while you're trying to work.

This is what Lisa Olson says happened to her while she was sitting on a stool interviewing a player in the locker room of the New England Patriots. News reports have tidied it up and called it sexual harassment, which makes it sound a little like some affirmative action issue. I'm giving the untidy version in the interests of accuracy.

Jocks have this tacit deal with the public. The deal is that they can get away with almost anything as long as they deliver the goods. One graduates from college barely able to read. Another gets caught driving drunk and mollifies the cop with an autograph. Yet another does drugs and after he comes out of rehab we welcome him back, and after it turns out he was lying about being clean we welcome him back again. We even had one ball player sent to jail for illegal gambling while fans contended that he deserved a place in the Hall of Fame.

Athletes are American princes and the locker room is their castle. Some of them behave in a princely fashion, become legitimate heroes to us all. And some are jerks. Jane Leavy, a former sportswriter for *The Washington Post,* has written a novel called *Squeeze Play* about a woman covering baseball and this is my favorite sentence: "You can't grow up if you spend your whole life perfecting the rhythms of childhood."

The other day Ms. Leavy recalled that the first time she interviewed Billy Martin, he was nude except for his socks and he had his feet up on his desk. This would be an interesting situation if you were a police reporter interviewing the police commissioner. Because you could describe this and then sit back and watch as the man lost his job.

Sports is different. That was just Billy being Billy.

Athletes are always testing, testing, testing. Some of them aren't good at finding the end zones in their own lives, which is why they test their bodies until their hamstrings snap, why they test coaches and owners until nobody wants them on their team, and why they test reporters. Particularly women reporters.

Some don't think women have any business being in locker rooms. With five hundred women sports reporters working today and the locker room still the place where reporters interview athletes, this view seems anachronistic. But it is a reasonable view if you believe the closest women should come to pro sports is the cheerleading squad or the backseat of a limousine.

Some also believe women are in the locker room for the express purpose of staring at what my sons, who have the same delusion of universal interest because they are small boys, call their "private parts." This is a red herring, this idea that somehow athletes must be naked in a locker room when reporters arrive. This week the coach of the Cincinnati Bengals decided to bar women from his locker room, a violation of law and of league policy, and said, "I will not allow women to walk in on fifty naked men."

Here's a tip, genius: Have them put on underwear.

Ordinary locker-room behavior doesn't have much to do with the organized harassment the league is investigating in the Olson case. And female sportswriters say lots of athletes are decent guys. The women sports reporters I know are very smart, smart enough to know who gets blamed for the sins of the jocks. At the Patriots game last Sunday, it was Lisa Olson the fans hooted.

This incident has changed her life, perhaps shortened her career as a sportswriter. Professional athletes know about short careers. Twenty years from now Lisa Olson will still be able to write, but there probably won't be one of the guys on that team who can still play football. Twenty years from now we will still have this bad bargain: You don't have to play by our rules as long as you perform. So long as you can dunk or pitch or block, you can get away with murder. Of course, when the legs and the arm are gone, all bets are off.

JOURNALISM
2001

April 12, 1992

I feel like one of those cartoon characters who have a little angel on one shoulder and a little devil on the other. The reporter— the one some people would say is carrying the pitchfork—says one thing, the human being another. There's a lot of this going around.

The subject is Arthur Ashe: the news is AIDS. This week the gentleman tennis player became a reluctant symbol. He had known since 1988 that he'd been infected by a transfusion, but he and his wife and a few close friends kept the secret for an obvious reason: they feared the shunning. Then someone tipped *USA Today*, and *USA Today* called and asked. Confirm or deny. That's how we do these things. Mr. Ashe called a press conference and went public.

Welcome to Journalism 2001. Anyone who tries to make readers believe the questions are simple ones, who automatically invokes freedom of the press and the public's right to know, is doing a disservice to America's newspapers and straining the credulity of its people. Naming rape victims. Outing gay people. The candidate's sex life. The candidate's drug use. Editors are making decisions they have never made before, on deadline, with only hours to spare, with competitors breathing down their necks.

I am disquieted by the Arthur Ashe story. I can't help feeling that in the medical sense we outed him, a practice that, in the sexual sense, I deplore. That's the human being talking. The reporter understands: public figure, big news. An editor argued rather persuasively on television that if Mr. Ashe had been in a car accident or been hospitalized for cancer, we would have written about it.

But listening to those arguments was like listening to others I'd heard not so long ago. We publish the names of victims of muggings, of murder; why not the names of victims of rape? The answer is that rape is not like other crimes. There are good arguments to be made that our newspapers shape our mind-set, and that by withholding the names of rape victims we perpetuate the stigma. You can make the same argument about reporting AIDS.

But, like the women who were raped, perhaps the victims of this illness deserve some special privacy.

Privacy, privacy. The white light of the press and the closed doors of our homes are two of the most deeply prized aspects of our lives as Americans. It just so happens that, just like those two little cartoon characters, they are often in direct opposition to each other.

Is Arthur Ashe still a public figure, this many years after his days at center court? If he is, need we know the medical condition of every public figure? If we are entitled to expose a reluctant patient, what about a reluctant gay person? What are the parameters? Mr. Ashe argued eloquently that he was neither running for office nor running a corporation, and that his health was no one's concern but his own. At a convention of newspaper editors, my colleagues argued otherwise.

I don't usually put this many questions in a column, but it's questioning that is going to serve the press best. Actually, there is no "the press." We are a collection of men and women, the good, the bad, and the nondescript. We know the dangers of knowing too little: we remember the Kennedy assassination, Watergate, Vietnam, and, more recently, the arid historical record of the Persian Gulf war.

We know about the man who was a member of the American Nazi Party and a leader of the Ku Klux Klan, who, in the face of a story that he had been born and raised a Jew, committed suicide. It was a very good story; the hypothetical is always whether you'd publish it, knowing the aftermath.

We tell people what we think they need to know. We hurt people, sometimes without reason. Sometimes we are kind. Mr. Ashe described a "silent and generous conspiracy to assist me in maintaining my privacy" on the part of some reporters. I would have joined up. This story makes me queasy. Perhaps it is the disparity between the value of the information conveyed and the magnitude of the pain inflicted.

But kindness is not the point. Information is the point of the product, and questioning the point of the process. We are making a lot of this up as we go along. In the newspaper business we assume certainty; when you spell Steven with a *v* it is because you know that's how Steven spells it. But we are moving these days into areas of great uncertainty. Arthur Ashe has already begun to turn his exposure into education. I hope we manage to do the same.

SUFFER THE LITTLE CHILDREN

July 26, 1992

Remember thirteen? Remember waking up in the morning never certain of exactly who you'd be? Remember being self-conscious about everything from your hair to your feet? Remember wild crushes, endless self-examination, stormy silences?

Corinne Quayle is thirteen. And she should be left in peace.

Oh, there was a certain satisfaction in watching what her dad did on television. Larry King personalized a question about abortion, asking the vice president what he would do if Corinne, when grown, discovered she was pregnant. The vice president launched into what abortion-rights advocates think of as the "my daughter" response.

People are troubled by abortion, even outright opposed. And then their daughter, their real daughter, not a poll question, not a hypothetical situation, turns out to be pregnant. And the world tilts.

That tilt is how Mr. Quayle, who has been an unwavering opponent of legal abortion, came to say of Corinne that he would "support her on whatever decision she made."

And that response is how his wife, Marilyn, came to say peremptorily, "If she becomes pregnant, she'll take the child to term."

And that is how I come to say "Enough." The right answer to Larry King's question was not about abortion but about privacy. Remember being thirteen. Imagine your mom and dad arguing on the national news about what they'd do if you got pregnant. Imagine P.E. class the next day.

Wow.

We have had one argument after another about privacy in this campaign. My sympathies have not been substantially aroused by the invasion of privacy that accompanies running for president.

But I feel for these kids. When I see Chelsea Clinton standing small at the center of the convention celebration, her braces glittering in the limelight, or when I think about Corinne Quayle being the most famous hypothetical in health class, the perimeters of privacy loom large.

I never liked Bill Clinton half so much as when, asked what he would do if Chelsea were pregnant, he replied, "I wouldn't talk to the press about it."

Political parents collaborate in this process. I thought Senator Gore was way over the line between illumination and invasion when he described his little boy's near-death experience in his acceptance speech. And I winced at the suggestion that Chelsea Clinton was upbeat about her parents' appearance on 60 *Minutes* during the Gennifer Flowers adultery brouhaha. At twelve, I didn't even want to think about my parents having sex with each other, much less with someone else.

I appreciate the balancing act. I've written about my own kids, wrestling with what is telling and what is merely tattling. The personal approach often yields the secrets of the heart; witness Larry King. But we have to count the cost.

The press exposure is not a new problem—ask Lynda Bird

Johnson Robb, who dated George Hamilton with a pop-eyed nation waiting up for her, or John F. Kennedy, Jr., who in some way will be forever three. But the kind of exposure is different now, tougher, more invasive, less fan mag, more social policy. Less fashion and dating, more drugs and abortion.

The exposure is so taken for granted that recently Linda Chavez, a former Reagan aide, suggested there was something odd about Chelsea Clinton's low profile during the primary season, as though political parents are suspect when they keep their children's lives private. Ms. Chavez remarked snidely that perhaps there was a problem, not with the quality of Clinton kids but the quantity.

"The one-child family is still the exception in America," Ms. Chavez said, "and I think that this whole image again sort of looks like the Democratic liberal version of what a family looks like."

There's a word for this kind of judgment. The word is "reprehensible."

I remember being thirteen. I remember how my mother would say "How was your day?" and I would think she was prying. No kid of that age should be pressed into service as a poster child. After years of lunches and train rides and shared beach houses we never learn so much about our friends as we do when we know their kids. Children are surely a character issue. But it's wrong to turn them into a campaign device. Remember thirteen.

A MISTAKE

April 21, 1991

I put my notebook on the kitchen table and pointed to the top line of a page.

"Who's that?" said my husband, looking at the name scrawled in my handwriting.

"The Central Park jogger," I said.

There were many of us in the news business who knew that name, and there were others in the financial community in New York City, her co-workers and classmates and clients, who knew it, too. I sometimes thought as many people in this big city knew that name as could populate a small one—say, Palm Beach, Florida. And we all had our reasons for not revealing it: some because they loved her, some because they respected her, some because their newspapers forbade it.

I fell into that last group, but I had another reason too. I did not use her name when I wrote about her because I thought it was the right thing to do. She had lost her balance, her memory, and, finally, on the witness stand, her anonymity. I thought that was enough. And I believed the reader lost nothing at all by not knowing.

Rape inspires very personal passions and this will need to be a very personal column, because it is also about *The New York Times*. Last week the *Times* made the decision to print the name of the woman who has accused William Kennedy Smith, the nephew of Senator Edward Kennedy, of raping her at the Kennedy family home in Palm Beach. Editors at the *Times* said the use of her name on an NBC news broadcast took the matter "out of their hands."

Her name was printed in a profile that contained the allegation by an unidentified acquaintance that she had "a little wild streak," what we in the trade call an anonymous pejorative, as well as the fact that her mother was named as the other woman in the divorce of a wealthy man she later married.

It included information about the seventeen traffic tickets she has received in the last eight years, as well as an anecdote about a restaurant chef who fixed her pasta after closing time, then was "disappointed" when she went to a bar with him and struck up a conversation with other men.

I imagined one of the editors for whom I have worked asking, "How does all this advance the story?" The answer is that it does not. It is the minutiae of skepticism.

There is a serious argument to be made about whether journalists should follow society or anticipate it, whether our refusal to print the names of rape victims merely perpetuates the stigma, or whether changing the policy would merely thwart prosecutions and shatter lives.

If we were to change that policy, there could not be a worse case in which to do so than this one. For NBC to change it in a case involving one of America's most powerful families inevitably suggested that the alleged victim had lost her privacy because of the Kennedy prestige. For *The New York Times*, a paper that has been justly proud of taking the lead on matters of journalistic moment, to announce that it was forced to follow was beneath its traditions. To do so in a story that contained not only the alleged victim's "wild streak" but the past sexual history of her mother could not help suggesting that the use of the name was not informative but punitive.

In the face of what we did in the Central Park case, the obvious conclusion was that women who graduate from Wellesley, have prestigious jobs, and are raped by a gang of black teenagers will be treated fairly by the press. And women who have "below average" high school grades, are well known at bars and dance clubs, and say that they have been raped by an acquaintance from an influential family after a night of drinking will not.

If we had any doubt about whether there is still a stigma attached to rape, it is gone for good. Any woman reading the *Times* profile now knows that to accuse a well-connected man of rape will invite a thorough reading not only of her own past but of her mother's and that she had better be ready to see not only her name but her drinking habits in print. I hope that the woman in Palm Beach, whose name I will not, need not, use, had some sense, however faint, of the pressures she would face. It could not have been a fully informed decision. I have been in the business of covering news for all my adult life, and even I could not have predicted this. Nor would I have wanted to.

KIDS
AND
ANIMALS

———————————————— ||–||–|| ————————————————

W. C. Fields hated to work with kids and animals; he said they always stole the spotlight. It's different for a writer, particularly one who has kids and animals just hanging around the house waiting to be scrutinized. It never occurred to me not to write about my children when I started doing a column called "Life in the 30s" in 1986; first of all, I was writing about my own life, and second of all, they were all I had to work with. When I was tending a twenty-month-old and nursing an infant, I wasn't exposed to much on a regular basis except bib overalls, diapers, toilet training, and monosyllables. Hell, it was a big day when I combed my hair, much less thought about NATO.

But even I began to worry when I leaned over to my eldest one day, after he'd said yet another cute kid thing, and asked, "Can I use that?"

Because I retired from column writing with the birth of our third child, our daughter, Maria, some readers had expected the column I began in 1990, "Public & Private," to be "Life in the 30s II—the Daughter Also Rises." It turned out to be something different, more public policy, less personal life, and I know I disappointed a fair number of readers by avoiding my children for large stretches of time. In print, that is. In real life the opposite was true. One day the editor of a very prominent magazine wrote to say that she found me difficult to track down for lunches and panels and other hoopla; why, she wondered, did I have this need to shun the spotlight, to be alone? I replied that I was almost never alone and that the rearing of three small children did not allow much time for socializing. It barely allows time for two columns a week and the occasional long shower.

Although some of the readers were eager for me to reprise the kids, the dogs, and the husband, I was not. There were many reasons—I think columnists, like sharks, have to keep moving or die—but one of them was maturational. Two of my children can read now, and I do not want them to feel embarrassed by seeing themselves discussed in print for the edification of the public. I once talked to Phyllis Theroux, the wonderful essayist who has written regularly about her adolescent children, and she said that it's not what you think—that you write an entire column about puberty and your fourteen-year-old daughter gets upset that you described her wearing leggings when no one wears leggings anymore. The photographer Sally Mann has said that her kids do not mind the exposure, even when they are nude. Like Ms. Theroux, she said the greatest concern is looking like geeks.

But I didn't want to take the chance. Leery of exposing my three-year-old in print, I knew I couldn't do it to my teenagers someday. I remembered hearing my mother say "Good morning" and thinking about how vile was the invasion of privacy. And I liked my mother.

Which means, not that I have stopped writing about children, but that I write about them in a different way. They interest me more generally now, in the way society treats them and the protections they allegedly enjoy. When I hear about a little boy who has been beaten to death by his mother, I respond on many levels, but one of the most important, and the truest, is as the mother of little boys myself, little boys whose injuries routinely break my heart. When I consider abortion, I think of it in part as the mother of a daughter. The day the Supreme Court handed down its landmark 1992 decision affirming *Roe* v. *Wade* but upholding certain state regulations, circumstances dictated that I read the opinion sitting on the front stoop with Maria blowing bubbles beside me. At one point, overwhelmed by the eloquence of the sentiments about the freedom of women, I turned to her and said, "Honey, no matter what, you'll know your mom did what she could to keep women free." Three years old and full of herself, my daughter replied, "Oh, Mama, don't be silly."

Because they still say things like this, sometimes I still write about my kids, in ways that I hope will not embarrass them now or later. When I was pulling together a collection of my columns some years ago, I said I was worried about that, that the clippings would yellow and crumble but hardcovers were forever. I will always be grateful to my husband for his response. He said that our children would be lucky enough to be able to revisit parts of their lives through my work. And he said that one of the most mysterious things for many children was the question of how their parents felt about things, about sex and love and drugs and bigotry—not the broad outlines of their positions, but the nuance, the thought process, the history, and the background. He said that he thought it took most kids a long time—until they were adults, really—to figure out who their parents were aside from their position as personal adjuncts. "But it's all right there for our kids," he said, holding the galleys of the book.

I write about kids differently now, but for the same reason I did when I wrote about weaning and sibling rivalry instead of parental leave and abortion notification statutes. I write about kids for my own sake, so that someday I can tell my own that I did the best I could to enjoin those who clobber the defenseless and disregard the concerns of the young. I write about them as the surest way to find out what I'm really made of, just as having three children taught me that day by day, minute by minute. And if the collateral effect of that is that someday my children will read my words and think that I stood up for them in public as well as in private, I will be happy with what I've done.

THE DAYS OF GILDED RIGATONI

May 12, 1991

Breakfast will be perfect. I know this from experience. Poached eggs expertly done, the toast in triangles, the juice fresh squeezed. A pot of coffee, a rose in a bud vase. A silver tray. I will eat every bit.

Breakfast will be perfect, except that it will be all wrong. The eggs should be a mess, in some no-man's-land between fried and scrambled, the toast underdone, the orange juice slopped over into the place where the jelly should be, if there were jelly, which there is not. Coffee lukewarm, tray steel-gray and suspiciously like a cookie sheet. I get to eat the yucky parts. I know this from experience.

Today is Mother's Day, and the room-service waiter at the hotel is bringing my breakfast. No handprint in a plaster-of-Paris circle with a ribbon through a hole in the top. Nothing made out of construction paper or macaroni spray-painted gold and glued to cardboard. This is a disaster. Any of the other 364 days of the year would be a wonderful time for a woman with small children to have a morning of peace and quiet. But solitary splendor on this day is like being a book with no reader. It raises that age-old question: If a mother screams in the forest and there are no children to hear it, is there any sound?

It has become commonplace to complain that Mother's Day is a manufactured holiday, cooked up by greeting-card moguls and covens of florists. But these complaints usually come from grownups who find themselves on a one-way street, who are stymied each year by the question of what to give a mature woman who says she has everything her heart desires except grandchildren.

It has become commonplace to flog ourselves if we are mothers, with our limitations if we stay home with the kids, with our obligations if we take jobs. It's why sometimes mothers who are not working outside their homes seem to suggest that the kids of those who are live on Chips Ahoy and walk barefoot through the snow to school. It's why sometimes mothers with outside jobs feel moved to ask about those other women, allegedly without malice, "What do they do all day?"

And amid that incomplete revolution in the job description, the commercial Mother's Day seems designed to salute a mother who is an endangered species, if not an outright fraud. A mother who is pink instead of fuchsia. A mother who bakes cookies and never cheats with the microwave. A mother who does not swear or scream, who wears an apron and a patient smile.

Not a mother who is away from home on a business trip on Mother's Day. Not a mother who said, "You can fax it to me, honey" when her son said he had written something in school and who is now doomed to remember that sentence the rest of her miserable life.

Not an imperfect mother.

The Mother's Day that means something, the Mother's Day that is not a duty but a real holiday, is about the perfect mother. It is about the mother before she becomes the human being, when she is still the center of our universe, when we are very young.

They are not long, the days of construction paper and gilded rigatoni. That's why we save those things so relentlessly, why the sisterhood of motherhood, those of us who can instantly make friends with a stranger by discussing colic and orthodonture, have as our coat of arms a sheet of small handprints executed in finger paint.

Each day we move a little closer to the sidelines of their lives, which is where we belong, if we do our job right. Until the day comes when they have to find a florist fast at noon because they had totally forgotten it was anything more than the second Sunday in May. Hassle city.

The little ones do not forget. They cut and paste and sweat over palsied capital letters and things built of Popsicle sticks about which you must never say, "What is this?"

Just for a little while, they believe in the perfect mom — that is, you, whoever and wherever you happen to be. "Everything I am," they might say, "I owe to my mother." And they believe they wrote the sentence themselves, even if they have to give you the card a couple of days late. Over the phone you can say, "They don't make breakfast the way you make it." And they will believe it. And it will be true.

SUICIDE
SOLUTION

September 20, 1990

It was two days before Christmas when Jay Vance blew off the bottom of his face with a shotgun still slippery with his best friend's blood. He went second. Ray Belknap went first. Ray died and Jay lived, and people said that when you looked at Jay's face afterward it was hard to tell which of them got the worst of the deal. "He just had no luck," Ray's mother would later say of her son to a writer from *Rolling Stone*, which was a considerable understatement.

Jay and Ray are both dead now. They might be only two of an endless number of American teenagers in concert T-shirts who drop out of school and live from album to album and beer to beer, except for two things. The first was that they decided to kill themselves as 1985 drew to a close.

The second is that their parents decided to blame it on rock 'n' roll.

When it was first filed in Nevada, the lawsuit brought by the families of Jay Vance and Ray Belknap against the members of the English band Judas Priest and their record company was said to be heavy metal on trial. I would love to convict heavy metal of almost anything—I would rather be locked in a room with one hundred accordion players than listen to Metallica—but music has little to do with this litigation. It is a sad attempt by grieving grown-ups to say, in a public forum, what their boys had been saying privately for years: "Someone's to blame for my failures, but it can't be me."

The product liability suit, which sought $6.2 million in damages, contended that the boys were "mesmerized" by subliminal suicide messages on a Judas Priest album. The most famous subliminal before this case came to trial was the section of a Beatles song that fans believed hinted at the death of Paul McCartney. The enormous interest that surrounded this seems terribly silly now, when Paul McCartney, far from being dead, has become the oldest living cute boy in the world.

There is nothing silly about the Judas Priest case—only something infinitely sad. Ray Belknap was eighteen. His parents split up before he was born. His mother has been married four times. Her last husband beat Ray with a belt, and, according to police, once threatened her with a gun while Ray watched. Like Jay Vance, Ray had a police record and had quit high school after two years. Like Jay, he liked guns and beer and used marijuana, hallucinogens, and cocaine.

Jay Vance, who died three years after the suicide attempt, his face a reconstructed Halloween mask, had a comparable coming of age. His mother was seventeen when he was born. When he was a child, she beat him often. As he got older, he beat her back. Once, checking himself into a detox center, he was asked, "What is your favorite leisure-time activity?" He answered, "Doing drugs." Jay is said to have consumed two six-packs of beer a day. There's a suicide note if I ever heard one.

It is difficult to understand how anyone could blame covert musical mumbling for what happened to these boys. On paper they had little to live for. But the truth is that their lives were not unlike the lives of many kids who live for their stereos and their beer buzz, who open the door to the corridor of the next forty years and see a future as empty and truncated as a closet. "Get a life," they say to one another. In the responsibility department, no one is home.

They are legion. Young men kill someone for a handful of coins, then are remorseless, even casual: Hey, man, things happen. And their parents nab the culprit: it was the city, the cops, the system, the crowd, the music. Anyone but him. Anyone but me. There's a new product on the market I call Parent in a Can. You can wipe a piece of paper on something in your kid's room and then spray the paper with this chemical. Cocaine traces, and the paper will turn turquoise. Marijuana, reddish brown. So easy to use—and no messy heart-to-heart talks, no constant parental presence. Only $44.95 plus $5 shipping and handling to do in a minute what you should have been doing for years.

In the Judas Priest lawsuit, it's easy to see how kids get the idea that they are not responsible for their actions. They inherit it. Heavy metal music is filled with violence, but Jay and Ray got plenty of that even with the stereo unplugged. The trial judge ruled that the band was not responsible for the suicides, but the families are pressing ahead with an appeal, looking for absolution for the horrible deaths of their sons. Heavy metal made them do it—not the revolving fathers, the beatings, the alcohol, the drugs, a failure of will or of nurturing. Someone's to blame. Someone else. Always someone else.

CRADLE TO GRAVE

December 7, 1991

He still had a trace of those delectable cheeks that dominate the face in babyhood, those round apples just below his eyes. In the photograph he is smiling. Despite it all.

Adam Mann was on television this week. For fifty-two minutes his story unraveled in a devastating *Frontline* documentary made by a producer named Carole Langer. She had followed him from cradle to grave; in Adam's case, the journey took only five years. He was beaten to death in March 1990 for eating a piece of cake. The last frame of the film was the little boy, the cheeks still round, in his casket. The caskets for kids are smaller. They cost less.

Who Killed Adam Mann? the film was called. His parents were charged with second-degree murder. His father pleaded guilty to manslaughter, his mother to assault. Both of them are in jail.

But Adam Mann had a guardian, too, and that guardian was supposed to be the City of New York and its Child Welfare Administration. Ms. Langer met the Mann children for the first time in 1983 when she was doing a documentary on caseworkers who investigate child-abuse complaints. The child in that film was Keith Mann; in one fourteen-month period he would suffer fractures of the face, ribs, arms, and skull. From the moment he was born and held in protective custody in the hospital nursery, Adam, Keith's younger brother, would be part of the city's vast child welfare system.

Reporters who cover the Child Welfare Administration know the drill. When you call about a case you are given a boilerplate response: Because of state laws of confidentiality, officials cannot provide any information. We go through the motions but we know that it is in vain. And we know that, no matter what the intent of the state law, the effect of it is to protect from scrutiny an agency that has historically served its citizens as poorly as any in the City of New York.

Ms. Langer obtained confidential documents on this case. To read them doesn't compromise these kids, Adam and his three brothers—it merely indicts the system that spends hundreds of millions of dollars every year, allegedly to care for children like them.

The Fatality Review Board report described caseworkers who failed to visit the home for months, who mistakenly filed the case away, who reported that the children seemed to be happy at around the same time that one was brought to the hospital, badly beaten, with a broken leg. Adam Mann's autopsy report detailed so many injuries that it looked like an annotated illustration from some medieval medical text. Doctors said that at one time nearly every bone in his body had been broken. His liver was split in two by his final beating.

The C.W.A.'s own confidential report concluded that the agency "completely failed to assess the nature, cause and seriousness of the family's problems and the danger to these children." No wonder it was confidential.

Who failed Adam Mann? A system that obviously needs a massive overhaul and independent oversight. A system that explains its failures to no one, even when its clients die. (In news stories about Adam's death, a representative of the C.W.A. "declined to say whether the agency was involved with the Mann children.") Robert Little, who has been its commissioner for a year now, says the Mann case "represents all that we came here to correct."

Adam Mann's mother is eligible for parole soon. A representative of the C.W.A. said at a recent hearing, according to those involved in the case, that it was the agency's intention to reunite her with her children. Commissioner Little says that decision will be made not by one person but by several. He talks about "family-friendly" procedures, and I think about broken bones. If Michelle Mann gets her children back, will there be regular visits from a caseworker? Will there be family therapy?

Will someone mistakenly put the file into the out box or become so overworked that, once again, the Mann children will become regular visitors to the emergency room? Will these kids, who are so damaged that one says he wants to join his brother in Heaven and another has run in front of a car, finally manage to keep a light burning in someone's mind? Who killed Adam Mann? And did anyone learn anything from his death within the system that so grievously failed him?

WITH BABIES
ON BOARD

June 3, 1990

They say that travel broadens a person, and I believe it. This may seem strange, considering that I have gone beyond the continental boundaries of the United States only twice in my life. Once I spent two weeks on the Caribbean island of St. Barts, which was a little like going to heaven. Once I spent two weeks in the Soviet Union, which was a little like going to Mars.

Nevertheless I have traveled a good deal, most of it in a large car with small children. None of the three children currently traveling with me are babies, although as recently as last year one of them was. There are two kinds of baby travelers. One kind equates the rumble of a moving car with the constant quiet stirring of the amniotic fluid. These are called ignition babies, and they are crackerjack travelers. You can turn the key in the ignition, and at precisely the same moment the engine will turn over and the baby will fall asleep, its big head flopping onto its bandy chest so that it looks even more misshapen than usual.

Then you can drive from New York to L.A. by way of Tahoe and never hear from this baby until you're pulling into the parking lot at the Beverly Hills Hotel.

The other kind of baby is called The Baby from Hell. You know. We had one, but she grew up. Otherwise I would have stayed home.

I cross state lines for the purposes of rural adventure with these three children twice a week, and a broadening experience it is indeed. There are many scenic attractions you visit with children that you never get to see when you are just a married couple and think the Jacuzzi in the hotel room is a relaxation device, not the home base for King Kruger the No. 1 Avenging Water Commando Who Wants to Make His Brother Cry. Frequently I have visited places that I would never have seen without the children, like the Land of Make Believe, the Blue Mountain Snake and Turtle Museum, assorted country fairs, and every McDonald's between New York and Scranton.

I have also seen the inside of many men's rooms since my sons reached the age at which they refused to use a toilet hiding behind a door with the silhouette of a woman's head. Mostly I have gone to the kind of places I first visited thirty years ago, traveling in a big yellow bus with a signed permission slip. These trips are just about the same today, except that I have to carry money. I still get sick on the Tilt-A-Whirl, I still can't knock over three suspicious-looking milk bottles with a hard ball, and I still can't see a damn thing in the World of Darkness exhibit. On the other hand, I can buy cotton candy with impunity because no one suspects it is for me.

All this has been very broadening, and I see lots of things that I would never notice otherwise. Such as:

"Oooooh, Mom, check out that deer on the side of the road. Look at its head, ooooh."

"Mom, how come that lady wasn't wearing a top to her bathing suit?"

"The kids in that red car have Fruit Roll-ups. If one of them tried to pass one over, can I take it?"

"Christopher, that raccoon is still there that got killed last week. Gross!"

The former Baby from Hell hoots along, then chucks a couple of stack-em toys at the back of my head.

"Cool!!!"

Of course this probably does not sound to you much like regular travel, which I am told includes gondola rides, shopping for couture, and lots of truffles, the kind that are chocolate and the kind that looks like something a dermatologist should be dealing with. But I have found that even in the course of regular travel children often transform the experience. For example, this spring these three children went on a trip to our nation's capital. It was the weekend when the cherry blossoms were in full bloom, and every family in America had taken its kids to Washington. It so happened that all of them chose to gather at lunch Saturday in the cafeteria at the Natural History branch of the Smithsonian. After the Smithsonian, we had our choice of the Washington Monument, the Capitol, the White House, Mount Vernon—the whole "This land is my land" routine. We decided to leave the decision-making up to the kids. (NOTE: Do not try this at home!)

"Room service!" shouted the second child.

"Good choice," said the first. "I've had room service, and room service was good."

So the high point of Washington was $14 pancakes and the ability to run back and forth for simultaneous viewing of the Smurfs on the television in the bedroom and Chip N'Dale on the one in the living area.

You can certainly see that this is a unique perspective on the sights and sounds of America, but it is not what is most broadening about my travel with these children. Incredibly, both boys were ignition babies, and so they seem to have a special spiritual feeling for riding in the car. While once the gentle swaying and strangled *whoosh-whoosh* of the ventilation system elicited sleep, now it clearly puts them in touch with their deepest selves, their hopes, their dreams, their karma if you will (I won't). So that it is commonplace to be driving along a superhighway, looking into the rearview mirror to see whether the state police car hiding behind that hillock has put on its cherry lights, to hear a small voice say:

"Mom, remember the sperm—"

(See trip from Pennsylvania to New Jersey in a driving snowstorm with frozen windshield wipers, Part 1.)

"—and the egg—"

(See bumper-to-bumper traffic occasioned by jackknifed tractor trailer complicated by Baby from Hell Cuts Teeth.)

"Well, how does the sperm get with the egg in the first place?"

Even before this sentence draws to a close I know that I must put my foot on the brake, since there is sure to be an accident ahead that I must maneuver around while explaining the miracle of conception. Sure enough, a Volvo has rear-ended a truck filled with Virginia hams.

"Cool," says the same voice. "How come something like that has never happened to us? Mom, can we go to Great Adventure tomorrow?"

"No."

"The Living Historical Farm?"

"No."

"Burger King?"

"Maybe."

I wait for the continuation of the sperm-and-egg conversation. Suddenly:

"Christopher, I smell skunk!"

The rip of rending Velcro tears through the back of the car as the former Baby from Hell removes her pink sneakers. Children in the car ahead of us flash the peace sign and the finger. If I were alone in this car I might not even notice them, or the possum that bought it at the curve up ahead. It occurs to me that I now look at the world a little the way David Lynch does. I look down at my gas gauge. The needle points to "empty." "Mom, when the sperm and the egg get together . . ." begins a voice from the back, and I reflexively put my foot on the brake.

RABBIT PUNCH

April 15, 1991

It is a difficult thing to rise up and decry those traditions and symbols that have become national customs. Although it is widely accepted that Mother's Day is a tool of crass commercial interests, a man attacks it (or forgets it) at his peril. Those lone voices that complain about the joylessness of Christmas are silenced by the rum-pum-pum-pum of Muzak carols in elevators.

Little attention was paid to the courage of one man, Calvin Trillin, when he suggested, a dozen years ago, that we stop talking turkey on Thanksgiving. Mr. Trillin was an eloquent representative of those of us who believe that, in taste tests, Americans served erasable bond with gravy and stuffing will swear it is good. The so-called Trillin movement to substitute spaghetti carbonara for turkey as the national harvest-feast dish has gone nowhere, except that there are now photographs of the man in the barns of many poultry farms, above the feed bin, with orders to peck to kill.

So it was not easy to make the decision to publicly trash the

Easter Bunny. The Easter Bunny has always troubled me. Santa Claus stands for giving, warmth, the magic of childhood.

The Easter Bunny stands for sugar.

I embrace tradition, custom, legend. I believe that children should have grounding in those events that make the year go round: their birthdays, my birthday, the first day of trout season, opening day at Yankee Stadium. And I believe in family myths and legends, those small moments, preserved in the amber of memory, that give a sense of continuity to life, like that wacky afternoon when Mom drove the wrong way down Eighth Avenue after she found the Jello-O Jigglers in her purse.

But the Easter Bunny is so unsatisfactory a holiday icon that no one even knows what he does. Does he color the eggs? Lay the eggs? Hide the eggs? What is his visual image? Is he a human-size rabbit (terrifying) or an average-size rabbit (well, then, how does he carry baskets?)? Some people imagine him wearing a pale blue velvet jacket. This is in fact Peter Rabbit, *not* the Easter Bunny; the confusion is a function of the fact that people think all rabbits look alike. A few people imagine the Easter Bunny wearing a top hat; these are readers of men's magazines.

What about transportation? Santa has a sleigh, the Tooth Fairy has wings. How does the Easter Bunny get from house to house? I have a child here who thinks the Easter Bunny drives a pickup truck. What kind of holiday symbol could conceivably drive a pickup truck? The Easter Bubba?

Background material is scanty. Most books note that the hare was a symbol of fecundity in ancient times.

Fecundity . . . chocolate . . . dyed chicks—oh, now I get it.

You know and I know that you can trace the rise of the Easter Bunny directly back to the rise of candy manufacturing in the United States. I support candy manufacturing. The only part of a chocolate rabbit I have no use for is the empty space in the center, and, of course, the best part of Easter is eating your children's candy while they are sleeping and trying to convince them the next morning that the chocolate rabbit came with one ear.

But all this is very confusing to today's children, who are always being fed things like kale. They meander along, living their whole-wheat lives, and then one Sunday they wake up and discover there is nothing on the menu but jellybeans and ham. I was so struck by this contrast that I once prepared a politically correct Easter basket filled with lovely bath surprises. The child's father peeked inside and said, "Duck soap?" in a tone of derision. And that was that.

Mr. Trillin advises that messing with the holidays is risky business and brings reader mail. He reports that even more unpopular than his Thanksgiving attack on turkey was his Christmas attack on fruitcake. Mr. Trillin likes to say that no one has ever been known to sigh, "Boy, I could really go for a piece of fruitcake right now." And he is right. I have insulated my family from fruitcake, but not from the Easter Bunny. Once a year some child has the wit to say, "Cool! He brought all the stuff that she never lets us eat!" Fecundity . . . plastic grass . . . marshmallow chicks—fill me in here.

ANOTHER KID IN THE KITCHEN

April 15, 1990

It is crowded in the kitchen. In a corner the baby leans back in her walker, gumming a biscuit. In another a toddler is eating Alphabits. A teenage boy, a skyscraper to the little ones, passes through with that sullen silence teenage boys own. A teenage girl, her hair a corn-colored tail down her back, scoops ice cream at the counter.

The mother of them all sits at the table, getting through the day on tea and cigarettes. The only one of her children missing is the middle one, the four-year-old, Melissa, nicknamed Sassy, known to the world as Baby M.

"I got the celebrity status without having a celebrity life," said Mary Beth Whitehead-Gould.

It's hard to believe, in this pretty, child-choked house on Long Island, that this woman blew her life to bits for the sake of another kid in the kitchen. The teenagers, Tuesday and Ryan, are Mary Beth's children by her first marriage. Austin and Morgan, the little ones, are the children of Dean Gould, whom she married three years ago.

And Sassy is the child of contract. Mary Beth was inseminated in an arrangement with Bill Stern, a biochemist who was to pay ten thousand dollars when she turned the baby over to him and his doctor wife. When she decided it was unnatural to do so, one of the nastiest custody battles of the century began. "It's a typical divorce," she said. "I have the kind of visitation fathers have — some weekends and a couple of weeks in summer."

Her credit cards say simply "Mary Gould," but she is recognized everywhere. Sometimes when she is out with Morgan, who is nine months old, people will whisper, "That's Baby M."

"They've frozen her in time," her mother says of Melissa. "To the public she'll always be a baby."

Public opinion is like that. We make up our minds and freeze the judgment, a leaf in the ice of the pond. There's no need to give it a second thought, except that those involved have to live with our first ones. "People are afraid of me," says the woman adjudged unstable by experts for pathology ranging from inadequate patty-cake to dyed hair. "I have to live with this reputation as an absolute wacko." This seems histrionic — one diagnosis at the trial — until three of my friends ask the same question: Is she nuts?

Well, she uses a lot of Windex and she seems a little obsessed with floral wallpaper, but her sanity is clear. Public opinion is sometimes wacko, too. While feminists were insisting that surrogacy was the exploitation of poor women by rich ones, I saw Mary Beth Whitehead as the have, and the Sterns as the have-nots. She had kids; they didn't. I sided with the Sterns.

I was wrong. I figured that out after reading Mrs. Gould's surprisingly eloquent book about the New Jersey Supreme Court's predictably eloquent decision. In one sentence it became clear: "We do not know of, and cannot conceive of, any other case where a perfectly fit mother was expected to surrender her newly born infant, perhaps forever, and was then told she was a bad mother because she did not."

Mary Beth is bound by court order not to talk about Melissa, but you can tell that the polarization of class and attitude so evident in the courtroom continues, though the rancor has subsided. In one household Sassy is the middle of five children whose thirty-three-year-old mother does not work outside the home; in another she is the only child of two professionals approaching middle age. Fruit Loops and cartoons in one place, raisins and the ballet in another. "Maybe it's the best of both worlds," says her mother, sounding unconvinced.

This is how public opinion works: People come to stand for something, and part of their humanity is forfeited in the process. Movie stars complain about this, but at least they get a house with a pool in the bargain, celebrity status, and the celebrity life. The ordinary folks who do extraordinary things face something more daunting. Norma McCorvey stood for legal abortion but had to have her baby because *Roe* v. *Wade* came too late. Karen Ann Quinlan's parents tended her for years after she became the symbol of the right to die.

And Mary Beth Whitehead has her daughter some weekends. Together they embody the false promise of surrogacy. "There's a piece of me that wishes it never happened," she says. "My children may meet people they'll want to marry and they won't be accepted because of who I am."

It would be good for everyone in the business of passing judgment, and those who do it as a hobby at the dinner table, to see her as she says this, staring out into a backyard full of toys, wondering whether her children will have to give up someone they love because once, in the white glare of the world court, their mother refused to do the same. "Time heals," she said. Scars stay.

MEN AT WORK

February, 18, 1992

Overheard in a Manhattan restaurant, one woman to another: "He's a terrific father, but he's never home."

The five o'clock dads can be seen on cable television these days, just after that time in the evening the stay-at-home moms call the arsenic hours. They are sixties sitcom reruns, Ward and Steve and Alex, and fifties guys. They eat dinner with their television families and provide counsel afterward in the den. Someday soon, if things keep going the way they are, their likenesses will be enshrined in a diorama in the Museum of Natural History, frozen in their recliner chairs. The sign will say, "Here sit lifelike representations of family men who worked only eight hours a day."

The five o'clock dad has become an endangered species. A corporate culture that believes presence is productivity, in which people of ambition are afraid to be seen leaving the office, has lengthened his workday and shortened his homelife. So has an economy that makes it difficult for families to break even at the end of the month. For the man who is paid by the hour, that means never saying no to overtime. For the man whose loyalty to the organization is measured in time at his desk, it means good-bye to nine to five.

To lots of small children it means a visiting father. The standard joke in one large corporate office is that the dads always say their children look like angels when they're sleeping because that's the only way they ever see them. A Gallup survey taken several years ago showed that roughly 12 percent of the men surveyed with children under the age of six worked more than sixty hours a week, and an additional 25 percent worked between fifty and sixty hours. (Less than 8 percent of the working women surveyed who had children of that age worked those hours.)

No matter how you divide it up, those are twelve-hour days. When the talk-show host Jane Wallace adopted a baby recently, she said one reason she was not troubled by becoming a mother without becoming a wife was that many of her married female friends were "functionally single," given the hours their husbands worked. The evening commuter rush is getting longer. The 7:45 to West Backofbeyond is more crowded than ever before. The eight o'clock dad. The nine o'clock dad.

There's a horribly sad irony to this, and it is that the quality of fathering is better than it was when the dads left work at five o'clock and came home to café curtains and tuna casserole. The five o'clock dad was remote, a "Wait till your father gets home" kind of dad with a newspaper for a face. The roles he and his wife had were clear: she did nurture and home, he did discipline and money.

The role fathers have carved out for themselves today is a vast improvement, a muddling of those old boundaries. Those of us obliged to convert behavior into trends have probably been a little heavy-handed on the shared childbirth and egalitarian diaper-changing. But fathers today do seem to be more emotional with their children, more nurturing, more open. Many say, "My father never told me he loved me," and so they tell their own children all the time that they love them.

When they're home.

There are people who think that this is changing even as we speak, that there is a kind of perestroika of home and work that we will look back on as beginning at the beginning of the 1990s. A nonprofit organization called the Families and Work Institute advises corporations on how to balance personal and professional obligations and concerns, and Ellen Galinsky, its cofounder, says she has noticed a change in the last year.

"When we first started doing this the groups of men and of women sounded very different," she said. "If the men complained at all about long hours, they complained about their wives' complaints. Now if the timbre of the voice was disguised I couldn't tell which is which. The men are saying: 'I don't want to live this way anymore. I want to be with my kids.' I think the corporate culture will have to begin to respond to that."

This change can only be to the good, not only for women but especially for men, and for kids, too. The stereotypical five o'clock dad belongs in a diorama, with his "Ask your mother" and his "Don't be a crybaby." The father who believes hugs and kisses are sex-blind and a dirty diaper requires a change, not a woman, is infinitely preferable. What a joy it would be if he were around more.

"This is the man's half of having it all," said Don Conway-Long, who teaches a course at Washington University in St. Louis about men's relationships that drew 135 students this year for thirty-five places. "We're trying to do what women want of us, what children want of us, but we're not willing to transform the workplace." In other words, the hearts and minds of today's fathers are definitely in the right place. If only their bodies could be there, too.

THE WAITING
LIST

November 16, 1991

It took four days to find a clown. Choco had a party already, Corky had a party already, Abracadabra had a party already, and Buster had a family emergency.

A friend passed on the number of Marcia the Musical Moose. "Hello," said the machine, "you've reached the home of Marcia the Musical Moose. My animal puppet friends and I aren't home right now—we're out grazing." Marcia the Musical Moose passed on the numbers of four other clowns, all female. I had visions of women clowns getting together in support groups, talking about how male clowns get all the good gigs. Marcia the Musical Moose was gentle but firm. "You're a little late," she said.

The real problem is that I am right on time. I was born in 1952 and my daughter is not going to have a clown at her birthday party. Pin the tail on the baby boom. Somewhere between a third and a quarter of all people living in America today were born between 1946 and 1965 and if you think you're tired of hearing about us, you should try being one of us.

It's been one waiting list after another, from the time they ran out of saddle shoes in the third grade to the back order for the bunk beds for the boys. Never alone. "Nora Ephron already wrote about this," said a friend. See what I mean? I have derivative thoughts, I'm on a waiting list for a clown, and I have a bad cold. "Oh, that cold," another friend said. "Everyone has that cold."

I watched the runners come out of the starting gate for the New York City marathon and swore I saw at least a few of the people who applied for my first job. Those were in the halcyon days when you'd go to see an apartment and there would be six other people looking. "Were you at the march on Washington in 1970?" one would say. We'd part, familiar strangers, only to meet again in Lamaze class (June of '83) or the headhunter's office (crash of '87).

There was the afternoon in 1986 when 2.4 million of us, all with Jeeps and roof racks, moved out of America's cities to the suburbs at one time, all vowing to come back frequently for the theater and dinners in Chinatown. It was like watching birds migrate, if birds shopped Ikea.

More white Haitian cotton sofas were sold between the years 1975 and 1985 than at any other time in our nation's history. An adaptable retailer, who could go from rolling papers to framed posters to collapsible strollers to relaxed-waist jeans, could make a bundle. No one has properly tied the boom in weight-reduction programs and hair weaving to the fact that one out of five Americans was attending a high school or college reunion sometime in the last decade.

My mother told me about sex, but not about demographics: Look, we all went a little crazy between D-Day and the Kennedy administration, and therefore you are never going to order from a catalog without having the items you want be out of stock.

My kids have a right to know. They are part of a baby boomlet that began in 1978. No one knows how big it will finally turn out to be; all we know is that when we lent out our maternity clothes they went around more times than a chain letter, and for years the vocabularies of everyone we knew were confined to these words: Aprica, Isomil, Nuk. If you yell "Kate!" in a crowded Kiddie City, there's a stampede.

I heard of a woman who was on a waiting list to have her labor induced.

I'm going to tell my kids that none of this has anything to do with them personally, that it is inevitable that if there are 187 applicants for every one place at the college of their choice, someone—well, actually 186 someones—is going to have to go elsewhere, and that there will always be a line for the new Disney film. "Enroll now!" says the flier from day camp. If you call in January they say sadly: "Oh, it's too late. We already have Justin, Jason, Alexander, Christopher D., Christopher K., Matthew, Benjamin, Ben, and Jonathan. We can put you on the waiting list."

Thousands of little girls turn three this month, all of them named Elizabeth. I finally unearthed the number of Violet the Clown, who had played the living room once before and was, incredibly, available. "You cut it close," she said. Balloon animals are a growth industry. So is what *American Demographics* magazine calls "the anti-aging market." The makers of Metamucil must be pleased.

"You'll never get into a nursing home," warned a friend. Enroll now for the waiting list. Arthritis? Oh, everyone has that arthritis.

MOM ALONE

March 18, 1991

Last year Twentieth Century–Fox released a little film it made for around $18 million, which is lunch money in Hollywood. It was called *Home Alone,* and was about a small boy accidentally left behind while his family went to France on vacation.

You could tell it was a fantasy because his parents flew first-class and left the kids to their own devices in coach without being arrested by customs agents or spat upon by their fellow passengers, and the family lived in the kind of house you dream of owning if you ever win Lotto, with no fingerprints around the light switches.

Perhaps because it bore no relation to real life, except that two guys tried to rob the house just before Christmas, the film became a monster hit, with box-office grosses that are now just shy of twice the gross national product of Grenada. It also became controversial because it contains violence. The sole residue of *Home Alone* for my children has been a tendency to mimic the boy in the film by placing their palms on their cheeks and screaming, disconcerting those who have not seen the movie and boring those who have.

The movie made a great impression on me.

It reinforced my sense that people who make movies are always to one side of the right track, on what in real life would be called a service road.

There is nothing remarkable about a child taking over the house, eating ice cream, watching videos, and ordering pizza. The concept reminds me of the old question: Why isn't there a Children's Day?

Answer: Every day is Children's Day.

The movie that really needed to be made was different: *Mom Alone,* the story of a woman whose family goes to Disney World and leaves her accidentally in her own bedroom, where she finds inner peace and her manicure scissors.

Scene one: Mom goes into the bathroom and stays there undisturbed for five minutes for the first time in a decade.

Scene two: Mom eats dinner sitting down, without sharing it with anyone, especially anyone who begs to taste it, then spits it out and says, "How can you eat that stuff?"

Scene three: Mom reads a book that is not by Maurice Sendak.

Scene four: Mom sleeps through the night.

And when the burglars come, Mom says, "If you try that again you will get your head handed to you," in a voice so terrifying that the burglars flee. In Orlando, unwrapping the guest soaps in the hotel and putting them in the toilet while Dad tries frantically to call Mom (amusing plot twist: Mom has taken the phone off the hook), the children would recognize Mom's warning as one they have heard, and ignored countless times.

I have other ideas for women's films: *The Godmother,* in which all the Corleone sons have been gunned down and the daughters take the family legit with small accessories stores and a chain of birthing centers; *Dances with Mom,* in which a woman goes to the wilderness to find herself and discovers she's already pretty darn evolved, and *Bonfire of the Vanity Fairs,* in which a female investment banker almost hits someone in the Bronx, puts on the brakes in time, and has an epiphany in which she realizes she is wasting her life imitating crass men and what she really wants is to develop housing for the homeless.

Mom Alone alone would generate controversy. The Sensitive Men lobby would suggest that it denigrates fathers. This is in direct contrast to television, which has produced a number of shows reflecting those millions of families in which mothers have left to join rock 'n' roll bands and fathers are left caring for their children alone, humorously.

The organization that Phyllis Schlafly runs, whose name always slips my mind, would say that no mother would want to spend a vacation alone beneath the down comforter watching *Waterloo Bridge* and eating Oreos when she could grab a plane and be standing in line at the Magic Kingdom that very day.

Uh-huh.

None of that will matter to movie people. All they care about are the grosses and the sequel. They're already planning a sequel to *Home Alone* and if I know that inventive industry that brought us *Beverly Hills Cop II,* it'll be a lot like the first, except terrible. (The kid will put his palms on his cheeks and scream again. Trust me.)

Mom Alone—Again. Scene one: Mom winds up on the wrong plane on her way to Sea World and goes to LaCosta, where she has a pedicure and gets to finish some sentences.

It's not a reality-based film like, say, *Pretty Woman.* But there's an audience out there.

BABES IN TOYLAND

July 31, 1991

The news that Barbie had been caught shoplifting sent shock waves through the world of little girls.

"Why did she do it?" said one. "Barbie had everything. She had jumpsuits, business suits, and an astronaut uniform with a lavender helmet. She had a Corvette, a beach cottage, and Ken."

Quickly I riffled through the newspaper, where there was a sidebar to the main arrest story by a child psychologist: "Barbie's Booboo—What to Tell Your Children." It said that petty theft often masked deeper problems and was a cry for help.

"It was a cry for help," I said. "A manifestation of some need, perhaps unmet in childhood, for affection and a feeling of belonging."

I thought of Barbie, with her impassive feline face and one-and-a-quarter-inch waist. I wasn't buying it. I explained that it might have been a mistake, that Barbie might have slipped those pantyhose into her Sun-n-Fun tote bag intending to pay for them, and then had just forgotten. It occurred to me that Barbie might have been set up by foreign toy manufacturers who wanted to flood the market with cheap imitations, dolls named Ashley or Melissa with lounge-singer wardrobes and boyfriends named Rick.

Like so many parents, I had learned my lesson from the Pee-wee Herman scandal of 1991. Over the years, the people in children's television have usually fallen into one of three categories: father (Captain Kangaroo, Jim Henson), puppet (Big Bird, Lamb Chop), or animated (Daffy Duck, et al.). Despite the suggestion by the Reverend Donald Wildmon some years back that Mighty Mouse appeared to be snorting cocaine in a cartoon, these characters rarely get in trouble with the law.

But Pee-wee Herman was none of these. Suddenly that summer there were stories everywhere telling parents how to explain to children that the weird little guy in a bow tie and lipstick who appeared on Saturday-morning TV with a talking chair and a pet pterodactyl had wound up in the clink, charged with exposing himself in a triple X movie theater.

At seven one morning, looking at the tabloids, I knew that before my first cup of coffee I was going to have to face two small boys and explain the difference between cartoon characters and real life, a difference I was a little fuzzy on myself, having lived through the Reagan years. So I did what anyone would do under the circumstances: I hid the papers.

"If they don't get their questions answered by their parents, where will they?" one child psychologist said to a wire-service reporter.

Simple: They'll get their questions answered on street corners and in the back of the bus to day camp.

After archery, I did explain the difference between characters and the actors who play them, the difference between being arrested and being convicted, the difference between private and public behavior, as well as the rules for keeping your pants on, which I can assure you we've been over a hundred times.

I explained that even grown-ups make mistakes, and that

despite published reports, what the actor who played Pee-wee was accused of doing was in no way comparable to mass murder, although in his mug shot he did look like a member of the Manson family. This made it easier for the kids to separate television and reality, although for a long time afterward they kept asking who played Peter Jennings on the evening news.

Pee-wee, of course, was history. This is a very unforgiving country, particularly after you've been famous enough to be made into a doll and sold at Toys 'R' Us.

So when the Barbie story broke big, it occurred to me that I might be witnessing the twilight of a career. I was not sorry. I had never wanted American girls to have a role model whose feet were perpetually frozen in the high-heel position.

Well, as you know, that's not the way it turned out. The next day Barbie's agent started spin control, and before you could say "dream house" there was a Sad-n-Sorry Community Service Barbie, with the navy blue shift and the open letter about how even dolls make mistakes. Little girls read it in the toy aisles and their eyes filled. "It wasn't a cry for help," I said. "It was a public relations stunt." But by that time the little girls I knew had gotten Community Service Barbie from their grandmothers, and they didn't care.

MOMMY DIMMEST

May 10, 1992

I think sometimes about a girl I met in Brooklyn. She was fourteen, and pregnant, and philosophical. "If Vanise does it, I can,"
she said, Vanise being the neighborhood dim bulb, the girl whose
conversation ranged from a giggle to a shrug, whose own mother
said that if you looked in one of her ears you could see daylight.

Vanise had had a baby, and she was so dim that it was commonplace for her to order a slice at the pizza place and then discover
she had no money and be obliged to cadge a buck from a boy.
(There was some suggestion of a causal relationship between the
slice, the cadging, and the baby.) The bottom line was this: if
Vanise could do motherhood, then motherhood couldn't be too
tough.

I guess the girl is nineteen now, and the baby five, and Lord
knows what happened to Vanise. I thought about them both, and
about all the rest of us who produce hostages to fortune, when
some manufacturer unveiled a pregnant doll called Mommy-To-

Be, a Barbie wannabe with country-western hair and a swelling midsection. What do you think it means that mine was delivered barefoot?

The doll reminded me of Vanise for two reasons: because it shows the world is full of people who don't have good sense, and because it suggests that having a baby is easy. It has a removable belly, and when you take out the baby—anatomically correct, which is a whole lot more than you can say about the mother—a nice flat stomach pops up in its place, thereby reinforcing the belly-button theory of birth so beloved by five-year-olds.

The process is a cross between a C-section, a tummy tuck, and an Easter-egg hunt. This isn't the way I remember it, but I guess there wasn't a big market for a sweaty wild-eyed doll with a hospital gown up around her armpits shrieking, "The next person who tells me to breathe is dead meat!"

It's always been this way. Our toys taught us that being a mother was simple. Betsy Wetsy, Tiny Tears—what easy babies they were. Today dolls are more sophisticated, but no more realistic. They have a baby doll that crawls and falls, but it does not fall against the leg of the coffee table, gash its little head and need to go to the emergency room at the same time that the twins are in the tub.

No Colicky Cathy, who wails all night unless you walk her. No Adolescent Alex, who does not speak for six months and then breaks the silence with a call at 1:00 A.M. informing you that he's gotten popped on a D.W.I. No real-life Mommy games.

(I never knew any boys to play Daddy when I was growing up. What kind of game would it have been to walk out the front door and make yourself scarce for ten hours?)

The job that seemed so easy when the babies were plastic turns out to be the hardest one you'll ever have when they're flesh and blood. The world is full of women blindsided by the unceasing demands of motherhood, still flabbergasted by how a job can be terrific and torturous, involving and utterly tedious, all at the same time. The world is full of women made to feel strange because what everyone assumes comes naturally is so difficult to do—never mind to do well.

No doll teaches this. The best exercise in understanding it is one sometimes given high school kids. They're handed an egg on a Friday and told that they have to take care of it all weekend. Most of them start with enthusiasm, naming their eggs, dressing them, drawing little faces on their blank whiteness.

But soon it begins to pall. They hunt around for someone to leave their egg with so they can go to the movies. Some of the guys try to talk girls into tending their eggs. One boy I read about hard-boiled his egg and then carried it around blithely in his pocket. I'm nervous about his prospects as a father, but I'm convinced he'll become a United States senator.

By Monday morning the eggs are broken.

We rarely admit that carrying something fragile with you, in your hands and your heart every minute of your life, is one tough task. I wonder sometimes how the fourteen-year-old and her dim friend wound up managing it, or if they did. The thing I find most annoying about this Mommy-To-Be doll is that she has a smile frozen on her face. Take off her big belly, pop out her baby, and she smiles and smiles. Motherhood is a snap. So simple. So easy. No stretch marks. No varicose veins. No potbelly. No problem. No way.

NAUGHTY
AND NICE

Dear Ms. Quindlen,

The other day at the mall a little boy passing by my throne said that if he didn't find Game Boy under the tree somebody was going to be in big trouble, adding a word that in my day was spelled *#!!@**&! What happened to the nice little boys and girls of yesteryear? Are there any left?

Be good for goodness' sake,
Santa Claus

Dear Mr. Claus,

Yes, Santa Claus, there is a Virginia. And despite everything you've seen on television and read in magazines, the amazing thing about her is how little she's changed since she asked for an orange in her stocking so many years ago. The boy you mention is exactly the sort who once would have said, "Your mother wears army boots." He would not have said it in front of you, however, because he believed that you knew who was naughty and nice.

The world they live in has changed plenty. Master Mall probably learned that word at home. A lot of us moms are more loose in our language than in the days when my mother once said "Oh, hell!"—she probably had just broken her toe at the time—and then clapped her hand over her mouth.

Our children's speech is anatomically correct, which seems like a good idea until the moment, in a crowded restaurant, when a two-year-old announces stereophonically, "Grandmom, I have a penis!"

Today's children inhabit a far harsher place than the world in which I waited for you each year. Five million of them under the age of six are living in poverty, which means that their toys may come via some church collection program rather than the traditional chimney route.

Fifty years ago teachers said their top discipline problems were talking, chewing gum, making noise, and running in the halls. The current list, by contrast, sounds like a cross between a rap sheet and the seven deadly sins: drug abuse, absenteeism, alcohol abuse, vandalism, assault, teenage pregnancy, suicide, gang warfare, rape, and arson.

But let's not fall prey to good-old-days-ism. Let's not pretend that none of the children you visited fifty years ago had abusive parents or empty stomachs. Let's not pretend that the world of Bedford Falls was perfect. I grew up safe, secure, and insulated in a suburb in which a Protestant was a rarity and a black family an impossibility. At this holiday season, my kids consider it one of my great shortcomings that I am ignorant of how to spin a dreidel.

This is a good thing.

They grow up faster, Santa. Too many of the Virginias of the world have babies when they are still babies themselves. Too many of them equate maturity with cynicism and hope with disappointment.

But there is a part of many of them, even some of the most superficially sophisticated or the most deeply scarred, that accounts for the continuing existence of you in a world that seems at odds with everything you stand for. It is that sense of infinite possibility, the genuine "Wow!" It is that sense that the blinds are not yet drawn between the windows of their eyes and the houses of their hearts.

The preternatural maturity we see in so many of them comes from us adults. It is our response to raising them in a world in which people die from sex and kill for pennies. It is to protect ourselves—we trade their innocence for street smarts for our own sake.

The Virginias of the world will tell you they want a Madonna cordless microphone and a pair of hoop earrings. But it is amazing how many of them still sleep with a tattered fur thing, part bear, part bunny. You may be conscious of how many of them no longer believe. I marvel at how many of them do.

I marvel at the pain it causes even the toughest customers to see beneath your beard and discover you are only a man in costume. It will be many, many years before some of them understand that you are a stand-in for what is best within themselves.

Those are the Virginias who grow wise but never weary. My New Year's resolution is to try to be one of them.

May your days be
merry and bright,

Anna Quindlen

ENOUGH
BOOKSHELVES

August 7, 1991

The voice I assume for children's bad behavior is like a winter coat, dark and heavy. I put it on the other night when my eldest child appeared in the kitchen doorway, an hour after he had gone to bed. "What are you doing down here?" I began to say, when he interrupted: "I finished it!"

The dominatrix tone went out the window and we settled down for an old-fashioned dish about the fine points of *The Phantom Tollbooth*. It is the wonderful tale of a bored and discontented boy named Milo and the journey he makes one day in his toy car with the Humbug and the Spelling Bee and a slew of other fantastical characters who change his life. I read it first when I was ten. I still have the book report I wrote, which began "This is the best book ever." That was long before I read *The Sound and the Fury* or *Little Dorrit,* the Lord Peter Wimsey mysteries or Elmore Leonard. I was still pretty close to the mark.

All of us have similar hopes for our children: good health, happiness, interesting and fulfilling work, financial stability. But like a model home that's different depending on who picks out the cabinets and the shutters, the fine points often vary. Some people go nuts when their children learn to walk, to throw a baseball, to pick out the "Moonlight Sonata" on the piano. The day I realized my eldest child could read was one of the happiest days of my life.

"One loses the capacity to grieve as a child grieves, or to rage as a child rages: hotly, despairingly, with tears of passion," the English novelist Anita Brookner writes in *Brief Lives,* her newest book. "One grows up, one becomes civilized, one learns one's manners, and consequently can no longer manage these two functions— sorrow and anger—adequately. Attempts to recapture that primal spontaneity are doomed, for the original reactions have been overlaid, forgotten."

And yet we constantly reclaim some part of that primal spontaneity through the youngest among us, not only through their sorrow and anger but simply through everyday discoveries, life unwrapped. To see a child touch the piano keys for the first time, to watch a small body slice through the surface of the water in a clean dive, is to experience the shock, not of the new, but of the familiar revisited as though it were strange and wonderful.

Reading has always been life unwrapped to me, a way of understanding the world and understanding myself through both the unknown and the everyday. If being a parent consists often of passing along chunks of ourselves to unwitting—often unwilling— recipients, then books are, for me, one of the simplest and most surefire ways of doing that. I would be most content if my children grew up to be the kind of people who think decorating consists mostly of building enough bookshelves. That would give them an infinite number of worlds in which to wander, and an entry to the real world, too; in the same way two strangers can settle down for a companionable gab over baseball seasons past and present, so it is often possible to connect with someone over a passion for books.

(Or the opposite, of course: I once met a man who said he

thought *War and Peace* was a big boring book, when the truth was that it was only he who was big and boring.)

I remember making summer reading lists for my sister, of her coming home one day from work with my limp and yellowed paperback copy of *Pride and Prejudice* in her bag and saying irritably, "Look, tell me if she marries Mr. Darcy, because if she doesn't I'm not going to finish the book." And the feeling of giddiness I felt as I piously said that I would never reveal an ending, while somewhere inside I was shouting, yes, yes, she will marry Mr. Darcy, over and over again, as often as you'd like.

You had only to see this boy's face when he said "I finished it!" to know that something had made an indelible mark upon him. I walked him back upstairs with a fresh book, my copy of *A Wrinkle in Time,* Madeleine L'Engle's unforgettable story of children who travel through time and space to save their father from the forces of evil. Now when I leave the room, he is reading by the pinpoint of his little reading light, the ship of his mind moving through high seas with the help of my compass. Just before I close the door, I catch a glimpse of the making of my self and the making of his, sharing some of the same timber. And I am a happy woman.

MR. SMITH GOES
TO HEAVEN

April 7, 1991

Jason Oliver C. Smith, a big dumb guy who was tan, died March 30 of lung cancer and old age. He was thirteen years old and lived in New Jersey, Pennsylvania, and the back section of the minivan, behind the kids' seat.

He was the son of somebody or other, but it was probably somebody with a name like Champion Snowfall's Big Brown Bear or Lancelot Smith of Sunnybrook. No one knew what the C. stood for, although there was speculation that, like Harry S. Truman's middle initial, it was an attempt to seem more dignified than he really was. He was called Mr. Smith only when he was reprimanded for eating the coffee cake off the kitchen counter and when he went to Washington.

He was born a golden retriever, although he never appeared in a Ralph Lauren ad, never gamboled through a field of daisies and high grass by the side of a slim woman with a picture hat in a television commercial for feminine-hygiene products.

He appeared in only one music video, *Twinkle, Twinkle, Little Star,* and fogged up the camera lens by licking it.

His pedigree was a source of some discomfort for his people, who acquired him just at that time when everyone who had been born between the years 1950 and 1955 and who had a four-wheel-drive vehicle and 2.2 children was acquiring a retriever. They were concerned lest other people think he was a status symbol. Luckily his behavior belied such a thing, and it was with great pride that they occasionally heard people say, "Gee, he acts just like a schnauzer."

With his passing, his people took stock of the relationship between man and animal and considered that people acquired dogs for the purposes of keeping in touch with their distant ancestors and of learning to remove hair from napped fabrics. People who wish to salute the free and independent side of their evolutionary character acquire cats. People who wish to pay homage to their servile and salivating roots own dogs.

(A friend and mourner recalled that, growing up, she believed cat and dog were the same animal, but that cats were the females and dogs the males. This is entirely credible.)

By human standards, Jason was a great success professionally. He was servile to the point of embarrassment, and was incapable of looking anyone in the eye for more than a few seconds, with the exception of insects. He frequently licked babies, and only an hour before he died he assiduously marked the trunk of a maple tree.

He was well known for his guilty expression, and on those occasions when he had rifled through the garbage it was not uncommon for him to look as though he deserved the death penalty.

His career as a retriever coincided with a period of cataclysmic change. The New York City dog-waste statute, commonly known as the pooper-scooper law, was enacted the year he was born. Late in life the animal rights movement swirled around him, and his master routinely threatened to make him into a coat.

His last illness came on the eve of the recent decision that stringent regulations governing pit bulls were discriminatory because they were breed-specific, and he seemed pleased when *My Life as a Dog* was critically acclaimed, although it was a little hard to tell since he was exhausted that week from treeing squirrels.

He lived in the city for most of his life, but he never wore a little plaid coat or a leather collar with fake gemstones, and he was never walked by a professional.

Although he began to visit the country only in middle age, he was able to find and flush quail, rabbits, and other small game. Nevertheless, he remained utterly incapable of getting within twenty feet of any of them.

At the time of his death his license was current and he had had all of his shots.

He is survived by two adults, three children, a cat named Daisy who drove him nuts, and his lifelong companion, Pudgy, whose spaying he always regretted, as well as a host of fleas, who have gone elsewhere, probably to Pudgy.

At the combined family Easter Egg Hunt/Memorial Service held in his honor, he was remembered by one of the children as "a really smart dog."

Unfortunately this was inaccurate.

Burial was behind the barn. A monument made of a piece of slate that had fallen from the roof was erected, bearing his name, a lopsided heart, and the initials of his people.

He will be missed by all, except Daisy.

He never bit anyone, which is more than you can say for most of us.

ON
THE
NEWS

T here are three questions people always ask about writing a column:

Q. Where do you get your ideas?

A. The same places that you do.

Q. How long does it take to write a column?

A. As long as I've got.

Q. How far ahead do you have columns stockpiled?

A. Say what?

All of those are wiseass responses, and all of them happen to be true. Because while sometimes columns come out of some strange area of expertise or personal exposure, while sometimes they are crafted over days of thinking and rethinking a subject, while sometimes they are written and then left in computer storage until an opportunity presents itself, most of the time newspaper columnists work exactly the same way they did when they were reporters—on the news, on deadline.

Each of us has subjects that are evergreen, to which we can turn whenever the engine of public discourse seems to have ground to a halt. There are books to be read and commented upon, habitual sources to be called.

William Safire, the conservative columnist who uses the telephone the way Leonard Bernstein once wielded the baton, does some of his most interesting work, as far as I'm concerned, when he simply calls his old boss for a long chat. His old boss happens to be Richard M. Nixon, and no matter what you—and I—may think of Mr. Nixon, there's no doubt that he is always good for some interesting thoughts on the state of geopolitics. Thus does Mr. Safire fill some of the arid spots magnificently.

But in my first two years of column-writing the dry spots were few, so few that I never once considered that perennial favorite among columnists, the column about the dearth of things to write columns about. The Gulf War was fodder for almost a year, from the time President Bush told Saddam Hussein that the United States could not stand quietly by while Iraq invaded Kuwait to the night when we went to war for the first time since I was still a student, to the aftermath in which many thought we had pulled out too soon, leaving Saddam still in power.

The 1992 presidential campaign was the same sort of cycle. It was not simply that these were obvious things to cover in a column. Sometimes they were the only thing. When the president actually authorized hostilities to begin in the Gulf, or when Gennifer Flowers told the world that Bill Clinton had been her paramour, it would have felt foolish to write about anything else, foolish to me, foolish to the readers.

Sitting in the faint glow of a computer screen, all alone in my narrow office, I flash from time to time on a coffee cup, a kitchen table, and a newspaper folded back to what I have written. The face of the reader is never really clear. Another ubiquitous question is whom I am writing for, and I often answer that given the size and scope of the *Times* circulation, and given the number of other papers that carry my column, if I tried to imagine the readership in my mind I'd go half mad. The truth is, the reader I write for is myself, which is the act of arrogance that powers the work of most columnists.

But whether I'm picturing myself hoisting that coffee cup, or seeing some faceless Everyreader instead, it is clear that there are days when there is only one story in the world, one thing that everyone is talking about, one topic that must be covered, about which readers, turning to the Op-Ed page, are saying, "Let's see what they think about that."

Perhaps no story in my first years as an Op-Ed columnist so clearly demanded that kind of attention as the one that emerged when Anita Hill, a professor at the University of Oklahoma Law School, temporarily derailed the nomination of Clarence Thomas to the Supreme Court—and turned the national agenda on its axis—by saying the nominee had sexually harassed her when she worked as his assistant. It is the only subject about which I have written four columns in a row without ever thinking I might be boring the reader. Whether you believed Professor Hill's story or not—and I did—and whether Clarence Thomas was confirmed or not—and, of course, he was—in the short but seemingly endless span of two weeks during which the story broke, the hearings were scheduled, the testimony from both sides was given, and the vote taken, there was simply no other story to be told.

When the details of Ms. Hill's allegations first began to emerge, I was not in my office, with easy access to wire stories and files, but in Albany on a reporting trip, with a full schedule of appointments and a column idea all ready for Wednesday. But I went to a dinner, and everyone said, "What are you going to write about Anita Hill?" Not: Are you? Not: Will you? To them, it was a done deal, the only thing on their minds. And that meant it must be the thing on my mind, too. That's how you know, whether you hear it from people at dinner, hear it discussed on the street, or hear it in your mind's ear.

Sometimes we do write columns that keep, but inevitably events like these intrude. Or the column begins to feel a little canned. Sometimes there are columns that can be cosseted into shape over days. But events like these unfold quickly, and luckily deadline work is second nature to most of us, even when we are analyzing the news instead of covering it.

(I cling to the rigors of deadline work when I look up and see one of my columns on the Gulf War tacked to my bulletin board. It was written just as the conflict drew to its triumphant close, and predicts confidently that George Bush will be reelected in 1992. It hangs there to remind me of the sin of hubris.)

And columns that must be written quickly as events unfold are often the easiest to produce. The Anita Hill columns were so deeply felt that by the time I actually sat down at the computer they were half written in my head. When I am deeply aggrieved I can never type fast enough.

How do I come up with column ideas? The same way you do, really, except that it is my job to do something with them. When you notice more people sleeping in the subways, you may shake your head and get on the train; I may do the same and then write about the worsening economy, or a street sweep in the bus stations, or the American anomie about pain and suffering. When your children learn to read, you may write it down in a baby book or file it away in your memory bank; I may do the same and then write a paean to Maurice Sendak, or a memoir about growing up a bookworm.

When Anita Hill spoke, all of us listened. And then some of us wrote. It really is as simple as that. Twice a week, week after week. Thank God for the news. I've felt that way my whole life, ever since I threw in my lot with the newspaper business. But never with more gratitude than now.

JUSTICE FOR THE
NEXT CENTURY

September 11, 1991

Picture a columnist appearing before an audience of readers. Someone asks a question about an issue—capital punishment, say, or abortion, or busing. And the columnist replies, "It would be improper for me to discuss that because I plan to write about it in the future."

Now, there's a considerable difference between columnists and justices of the Supreme Court, the greatest being that the latter are infinitely more important, despite what the former sometimes seem to believe.

The similarity is that the trade-secret response for either is insulting to the audience. Yesterday Senator Joseph Biden noted that Clarence Thomas would, if confirmed, serve on the Court well into the twenty-first century, and so it seems a good time to establish a twenty-first-century agenda for confirmation hearings. And that is what the American people should know and the Judiciary Committee should try to uncover: how a nominee thinks, how his mind works.

Clarence Thomas's biography has become the linchpin of his appointment to the Court—his impoverished childhood, his rise from humble beginnings. We know the color of his skin; now it is time for the content of his character and the caliber of his mind. We need to know not necessarily his intellectual and judicial destinations but the roads he will travel to arrive at them.

More than his personal opinion on abortion, I want to know what he thinks of the reasoning of *Roe* v. *Wade*. I hope the committee will continue to ask about that decision, about what he sees as its shortcomings and its strengths. I would like to know his thinking on privacy rights and the right to reproductive freedom.

I hope there will be many questions about *Brown* v. *Board of Education*, the landmark school desegregation decision that Judge Thomas has criticized in the past. I hope there will be many questions about his philosophy regarding sex and age discrimination, about affirmative action and the rights of the accused.

I hope he will be urged to speak publicly about the Constitution, about whether it should be interpreted narrowly or broadly, about how he would assess the work of Thurgood Marshall, about his judicial role models.

In a 1987 speech Judge Thomas cited "natural law" as the bedrock of the American political tradition, adding, "The thesis of natural law is that human nature provides the key to how men ought to live their lives." Yesterday Senator Biden said that natural law was the single most important issue before the committee. I hope someone will try to discover how Judge Thomas squares his belief in natural law with its historical use as a tool of discrimination, about whether natural law is just another name for personal or religious beliefs and what role such beliefs should properly play in the decisions of the Supreme Court.

The next justice of that Court should be not just competent but gifted. Judge Thomas does not have the judicial track record to make that manifest, and so the Judiciary Committee must do so now. It will not be done by pretending that the life of his mind is classified information. That attitude was concocted to protect not the stature of the Court but the nominee, who in giving a definite answer might give one that committee members would dislike.

One refrain is that nominations to the High Court are not and should not be political. That is a preposterous notion in light of the president's determination to nominate a conservative no matter how distinguished the liberal pool. But it also ignores the fact that politics is just another word for a way of looking at the world, and that a way of looking at our world is something we want to know about any high official whose decisions will change our lives.

The notion that nominees to the Court should not talk about matters of law assumes that what Justice Souter, at his own confirmation hearings, called "the promise of impartiality" is an absolute, and that judges come to us with a tabula rasa. The truth is that judges bring their past, their philosophy, and their political orientation to the bench. Sometimes they make decisions because of them, and sometimes in spite of them. That is their job.

The job of the Judiciary Committee, acting on our behalf, is to find out everything it can about those things, to labor mightily to reveal the mind within the man, for now and for the century ahead.

THE BLANK SLATE

September 14, 1991

Orrin Hatch seemed peevish. The Republican senator from Utah had determined that members of the Judiciary Committee had asked Clarence Thomas twice as many questions about abortion as they had asked David Souter a year ago. "You'd think from listening to what's going on here that that's the only issue the Supreme Court has to decide," he said.

Right on both counts: Judge Thomas has been questioned more closely than Justice Souter on *Roe* v. *Wade,* and there are other important issues before the Court in the terms to come. It was the senator's affect that was wrong, the way in which he seemed to suggest that the issue of abortion was a pesky fly buzzing around the room, an annoyance that should be either ignored or eliminated.

There are many issues the Supreme Court will take up come October, but none other has thrown an entire American city into turmoil this summer. None other has resulted in demonstrations and mass arrests in communities across the country. None other addresses the bodily integrity of half our citizenry. None other has become as controversial and as important as this one has. Whether Senator Hatch wants to slap it down or not, it is not going to fade away.

Watching the confirmation hearings of Clarence Thomas has been a sobering, sometimes saddening, occasionally illuminating exercise. A year ago Justice Souter was a cipher trying to take on intellectual flesh. Judge Thomas has been exactly the opposite—an opinionated individual with a rich and contradictory past and paper trail trying to present himself as a blank slate. "Stripped down like a runner," in his own words.

The controversial writings and pronouncements on affirmative action, natural law, discrimination—most, he suggests now, were misinterpreted, oversimplified, taken out of context. In the weeks leading up to the hearings we heard often of the strong-minded black conservative who disdained quotas and criticized his own sister for dependence on a welfare check. That man has been conspicuously missing, although from time to time behind the oh-so-intense eyes I suspect the Clarence Thomas with flammable opinions is yearning to burst loose. Then I see him sharing a few laughs with Strom Thurmond and think I am imagining things.

Nowhere has the blank slate been more unsatisfactory and unconvincing than it has been on the issue of abortion, which is, for some of us, the issue of our lives. It was not only that Judge Thomas repeatedly said he could not discuss the matter and maintain his impartiality, although he was strangely able to discuss other issues that will likely come before the Court. When he was asked to recount discussions he might have had in law school on the subject, he replied, "I cannot remember personally engaging in those discussions," and perhaps there were even people who believed him. He also thought for a long time when he was asked whether the fetus has constitutional status as a person. "I cannot think of any cases that have held that," he finally replied.

Quite the contrary. The operative sentence is: "The word 'person,' as used in the 14th Amendment, does not include the unborn." The case is *Roe* v. *Wade.*

There is occasionally a man at that table who might be capable of addressing this issue with humanity. He is the man who has presented such a problem for liberals in recent weeks, a man who knows from experience what discrimination and disfranchisement are all about. He is the man who said on Thursday that from the window of his courthouse he could look out and see the buses transporting criminal defendants, adding, "I say to myself almost every day, but for the grace of God, there go I."

I wish I had any confidence that he considered those of us who feel that way when we see a group of desperate women in a clinic waiting room. To watch as one of the most important issues of our times, an issue that intimately affects the lives of millions of women, is reduced to a political fandango in some cynical means-ends construct and a peevish annoyance for a senator who will never have to think twice about who holds jurisdiction over the territory beneath his skin is worse than dispiriting. It's insulting. A man in robes who is capable of looking at men in handcuffs and seeing himself ought to recognize that.

LISTEN TO US

October 9, 1991

Listen to us.

You will notice there is no "please" in that sentence. It is difficult to be polite, watching the white men of the United States Senate and realizing that their first response when confronted with a serious allegation of sexual harassment against a man nominated to the High Court was to rush to judgment. It is difficult to be polite, knowing they were more concerned about how this looked for them, for their party, their procedures, and their political prospects than in discovering what really happened.

The gender divide has opened and swallowed politeness like a great hungry whale. Why? Why? Why? they asked. Why did Anita Hill, now a tenured law professor at the University of Oklahoma, not bring charges against Clarence Thomas when, she contends, he sexually harassed her a decade ago? Why did she stay on the job although, she says, he insisted on discussing with her the details of pornographic movies? Why was she hesitant about confiding in the Judiciary Committee?

The women I know have had no difficulty imagining possible answers. Perhaps she thought no one would believe her, he being powerful and she not. If she was indeed humiliated by her boss in the seamy way she describes, regaled with recountings of bestiality and rape when she was fresh out of law school and new to the world of work, perhaps she decided it was best buried in her memory. Perhaps she thought the world would never believe that the man charged with enforcing sexual harassment laws as chairman of the Equal Employment Opportunity Commission would do such a thing.

From time to time I am told of the oppression of the white male, of how the movements to free minorities from prejudice have resulted in bias against the majority. Watching Judge Thomas's confirmation hearings, I wondered how any sane person could give this credence. The absence on the panel of anyone who could become pregnant accidentally or discover her salary was five thousand dollars a year less than that of her male counterpart meant there was a hole in the consciousness of the committee that empathy, however welcome, could not entirely fill. The need for more women in elective office was vivid every time the cameras panned that line of knotted ties.

"They just don't get it," we said, as we've said so many times before, about slurs, about condescension, about rape cases.

Judge Thomas has floated on the unassailable raft of his background—impoverished boyhood to Yale Law to public position, a rise that was impossible to diminish. Professor Hill had the same climb, with the added weight of gender. It seems obvious that she has been caught between the damage she feared these charges might do to her hard-won stature and the morality of watching in silence the elevation of a man she believes is capable of harassing women.

One of the most difficult things about bringing sexual harassment charges is that it is usually one woman against the corporate power structure, against not only the boss who says she's imagining things but also a bulwark of male authority that surrounds him. Davids against the Goliaths. Anita Hill, poised and dignified, spoke up Monday and found herself aligned against the most powerful men in America, including the president. Who among us would have had the guts to pick up her slingshot?

Listen to us. If the Senate had trivialized the allegations of this woman by moving ahead without painstaking investigation, it would have sent a message: that no matter what we accomplish, we are still seen as oversensitive schoolgirls or duplicitous scorned women. Obviously it would have been better if Professor Hill had stepped forward earlier, content to be reviled and be suspect in the public eye.

But I understand what she feared: that what has happened would happen. That the focus would be not on what Clarence Thomas did to Anita Hill, but on what Anita Hill did to Clarence Thomas, and who leaked it to the press, and why it's emerging now, and all the peripheral matters that make the central concern, the right to work unmolested, seem diminished and unimportant. The Senate has the opportunity, in the days to come, to prove that this is not a government by men for men. Listen to us. Listen to her. Then decide.

AN AMERICAN
TRAGEDY

October 12, 1991

"He said that if I ever told anyone of his behavior it would ruin his career."

—ANITA HILL

And he was right.

The members of the Senate Judiciary Committee sat in silence yesterday as their chairman led an obviously intelligent and thoughtful female professor of law through the first discussion of genitalia in the history of the Supreme Court confirmation process. The event was by turns seamy, surreal, and stunning, and was carried on all major networks in its entirety. It was the first time I have ever switched off the TV during a Senate hearing because my children had entered the room.

It was all there under the lights, as she told it, a case study of sexual harassment: the repeated requests for dates, the dirty comments, the fear of reprisals or firing, the repression. "Thomas told me graphically of his own sexual prowess," said Anita Hill. I knew what she had felt, what she was afraid she would feel if she testified, because I could feel it too. I felt soiled by the time they broke for lunch.

With her elderly parents, both farmers, sitting behind her, Professor Hill talked of working for Judge Thomas a decade ago, and of how he asked her out repeatedly and repeatedly discussed hard-core pornography. "His conversations were very vivid," she said. She recounted an incident in which her then boss discussed porno featuring a man with a large penis. Senator Biden asked gingerly if she could remember the name of the fictional character.

"Long Dong Silver," Professor Hill said, and at that moment the career of Clarence Thomas turned to ashes.

An American tragedy was on television yesterday. There was plenty of blame to be spread around. The Judiciary Committee has borne a great resemblance to the little car at the circus filled with clowns. You could not help wondering whether, if they had not acted differently, we might have all been spared some part of this—the people of this country, and Anita Hill, and Clarence Thomas, too.

The president is also to blame. A politician whose sole principle is pragmatism, he told the American people that he had chosen the most qualified man for the job, which was not true. He picked a man whose judicial experience was so meager, whose confirmation-hearing testimony was so devoid of substance, that he could be confirmed only on his character: Clarence Thomas, self-made man.

But Anita Hill spoke of the Clarence Thomas who made her life ugly, dirty, disgusting, who warned her in parting that she had the power to ruin his career. The committee members pressed her to be more graphic, but she went so far, and then no further. What a great relief that was, those moments when she compressed her lips and called a halt.

I suppose I should take note of the positive effect of this on the national consciousness. We have learned so much about sexual harassment in so short a time that Peter Jennings felt compelled to confide on the air that the men in his office had gotten an education in the last few days.

But yesterday was no time to stand up and cheer. Two human beings, both well spoken and handsome, both Horatio Alger stories, were forced to put their dignity and veracity on the line. Clarence Thomas made a powerful speech in which he called the confirmation process "Kafkaesque" and added, "No job is worth what I've been through." A half dozen times during his remarks he sounded as though he was going to remove his name from consideration.

The biggest mistake he made was in not doing so.

The good thing about writing an opinion column is that you can have an opinion, and my opinion is that Anita Hill is a credible witness and that Clarence Thomas is unfit to sit on the Supreme Court. I do not believe he is good enough. The Senate should have rejected him for that reason alone.

If they reject him now, history will record that he was rejected because he insisted on talking to his assistant about group and oral sex, large penises and large breasts. And it will record that he took our self-portrait with him. Anita Hill told us yesterday that sometimes women go to work in fear that they will have to listen to filth as part of their duties, that they put up with it because they need the pay or the recommendation, that their bosses may be among the most powerful and respected men in the country. She spoke calmly. She testified persuasively. It was a horrible thing to watch.

THE PERFECT VICTIM

October 16, 1991

She seemed the perfect victim. Or perhaps it is more accurate to say that she was the perfect person to teach us that there are no perfect victims, that no matter how impressive your person, how detailed your story, how unblemished your past, if you stand up and say, "He did this to me," someone will find a way to discredit you.

And so it was with Anita Hill. Intelligent, composed, unflappable, religious, and attractive, she testified to her sexual harassment by Clarence Thomas and even to her own inadequacies, agreeing that it had taken her too long to come forward, that it was hard to understand why she had kept in touch. And as soon as she left the room, she was portrayed as nut case, romantic loser, woman scorned, perjurer.

Clarence Thomas thundered about the sexual stereotypes of black men, and the Senate gasped obligingly. Little attention was paid to the stereotypes leveled at Professor Hill. Aloof. Hard. Tough. Arrogant. This is familiar shorthand to any successful woman. She wanted to date him. She wasn't promoted. She's being used by his enemies. This is familiar shorthand to anyone who has ever tried to take on the men in power.

African-American women are sometimes asked to choose sides, to choose whether to align themselves with their sisters or with their brothers. To choose whether to stand against the indignities done them as women, sometimes by men of their own race, or to remember that black men take enough of a beating from the white world and to hold their peace. The race card versus the gender card. Clarence Thomas milked the schism.

With his cynical invocation of lynching, he played in a masterly way on the fact that the liberal guilt about racism remains greater than guilt about the routine mistreatment of women. We saw more of Judge Thomas's character last weekend than we ever did during his confirmation hearings. What we learned is that he is rigid, anxious to portray himself as perfect, a man who will not even allow that two men watching a football game might talk differently than they would if there were women in the room.

The members of the Senate took to the floor yesterday and congratulated themselves on educating the American people about sexual harassment. Well, here is what they taught me:

That Senator Orrin Hatch needs to spend more time in the taverns of America if he thinks that only psychopaths talk dirty.

That the party of the Willie Horton commercials is alive and well and continuing to indulge in the deft smear for the simple reason that it works.

That the Democrats behaved in these hearings the way they have in presidential elections, hamstrung by their own dirty linen, ineffectual in their pallid punches, weak advocates for the disfranchised.

I learned that if I ever claim sexual harassment, I will be confronted with every bozo I once dated, every woman I once impressed as snotty and superior, and together they will provide a convenient excuse to disbelieve me. The lesson we learned, watching the perfect victim, is that all of us imperfect types, with lies in our past or spotty job histories, without education or the gift of oratory, should just grin and bear it, and try to stay out of the supply closet. "This sexual harassment crap," Senator Alan Simpson called it, evidencing his interest in women's issues.

What I learned from Professor Hill was different. When she returned to Oklahoma, where she may well teach all the rest of her days, unmolested by offers of high appointment because of her status as a historical novelty act, she had a kind of radiance. It seemed to me the tranquillity of a person who has done the right thing and who believes that is more important than public perception.

There is only one explanation for her story that seems sensible and logical to me, that does not require conspiracy theories or tortured amateur psychoanalyzing or a member of the United States Senate making himself look foolish by reading aloud from *The Exorcist*. There is only one explanation that seems based not in the plot of some improbable thriller but in the experiences of real life, which the members of the Senate seem to know powerfully little about. That explanation is that she was telling the truth and he was not. Simple as that. She got trashed and he got confirmed. Simple as that.

THE TROUBLE
WITH TEDDY

October 19, 1991

The trouble with Teddy is that he's like the little girl with the curl in the middle of her forehead. When he's good, he's better than anyone else, but when he's bad—oh, boy!

When he finally opened his mouth during the Judiciary Committee hearings on Anita Hill's charges against Clarence Thomas he tied it all up with a ribbon. He said with considerable ire that he hoped we would not be hearing any more about perjury or racism, that instead of trying to divert attention the committee should concentrate on sexual harassment. For just a moment he was what he was always meant to be: Edward M. Kennedy, the liberal conscience of the Senate. And then he lapsed back into a self-imposed silence, into the cat's cradle woven of the facts of Teddy's private life.

It was during the 1988 election that the great debate erupted over the impact of personal behavior on political fitness. Gary Hart. Donna Rice. Monkey Business. There were many who proclaimed that the private life of a public man is not the point and that the public had no need to know about behavior after hours.

I've never believed that. It is difficult for me to imagine the same dedication to women's rights on the part of the kind of man who lives in partnership with someone he likes and respects, and the kind of man who considers breast-augmentation surgery self-improvement. That was my argument in '88, that I had problems with the kind of guy who thundered against sex discrimination but couldn't keep his hands off women. And it continued to be my argument, as issues affecting the way we live moved to the forefront of national affairs.

Now I need not make the argument; all the world is making it. And one of the reasons they are making it is the trouble with Teddy, which has neutralized one of the ablest members of the Senate at the moment he was needed most.

Everyone knew why the senior senator from Massachusetts turned into an inanimate object when the hearings turned to the subject of sexual harassment. It was because of the split between his public and private selves, because of accounts of his drinking and his exploits with women, because of his nephew in Palm Beach and his car in Chappaquiddick.

Even one of his close friends stooped to conquer. Criticizing a remark of Mr. Kennedy's, Orrin Hatch said, "Anybody who believes that, I know a bridge up in Massachusetts that I'll be happy to sell to them." Later Senator Hatch apologized, saying he meant a bridge in Brooklyn.

And if you believe that, there is a bridge in Brooklyn I'd like to sell.

This is not a plea for perfect men in public life, although if there are any hanging around we could use them. Nor is it an affirmation of those women who believe that because the Democrats let us down, we should cut them loose. I understand the disenchantment, but if I have a choice between zapping any Democrat on the Judiciary Committee or, say, Alan Simpson, whose idea of investigation is to say he has lots of dirt on the witness and then to refuse to make it public—well, that's not a tough call.

But I do believe it is time for our elected officials to act like men and not overgrown fraternity boys who use political positions as the ultimate pickup line. And it's time for us to be realistic about the inevitable nexus between the personal and the political, about the essential contradiction between voting on issues that empower women and seeing them as inflatable dolls in private.

Wanda Baucus, an anthropologist married to the Democratic senator from Montana, revealed in *The Washington Post* yesterday that she has been sexually harassed by—surprise!—two members of the United States Senate: one Republican before she was married, one Democrat after. Asking such men to decide a question of sexual harassment is not exactly like having gun control decided by someone who's been known to enter a convenience store and spray the deli counter with bullets. But it's close.

Teddy Kennedy has, over the years, been the exception. Last week he proved the rule. Sex discrimination, family leave—we feminists have always felt he was on our side. He let us down because he had to; he was muzzled by the facts of his life. And he proved once and for all that the private life of a politician casts an indelible shadow over public affairs, sometimes to the detriment of the public.

THE INVASION
VACATION

August 19, 1990

We didn't want to take this vacation. It was the president's idea. I figured we should just call August on account of invasion, hunker down, and wait for the price of gasoline to reach the foie-gras mark. The president would have none of this. "The American people want to see life go on," he said.

This was not as easy as it sounded. As a patriotic gesture, we bought charcoal briquets and went to the middle of nowhere. The middle of nowhere was in the middle of the Middle East mania. News followed us to the outdoor art show and the Farmer's Market.

The Village Grocery became Democracy Central. First thing in the morning the bread-delivery man, the milk-delivery man, and the man who runs the place would be clustered around the cash register, trashing Saddam Hussein and tracking troop deployments. "I think the president is right on the money," they said. This is the kind of place where the president is usually right on the money.

The gas station was raucous with gas-line lore, much of it macho and apocryphal. Testosterone filled the air. War will do that. You know the drill: "Remember in '79 when you punched out that guy who tried to cut in line to put air in his tires, Phil?" someone says. "Hell," says Phil, "I never punched him out. I ran over his foot. And it was '73."

At the mall, teenagers in heavy-metal T-shirts sullenly absorbed current events. "Saddam Hussein, man," they would say, if they could talk. "He's toast."

America has rallied round, and it is something to see. There's a local angle, no matter what the locality—American kids in khaki, folks like us held hostage to empty gas tanks. The story is writ large: friends, foes, a big bad guy with the sinister mustache of a James Bond villain. The Iraqis have replaced the Soviets in the "evil empire" role, much missed since we began playing "I'm O.K., you're O.K." with the Russians. Polls show that Americans are more possessed by this story than by any in years.

People say it's hard to get away from it all because of the magic of cable television, fax machines, computer modems. But this time around it's democracy that's doing us in. Now that election campaigns bear more of a resemblance to MTV than to statesmanship, we've got two ways to reaffirm what this county stands for. One is the jury room, with its miraculous ability to turn twelve bumbling United States citizens into paragons of diplomacy, objectivity, and thoughtfulness.

The other is crisis management. Iraq invades Kuwait and—bingo!—all Americans become experts on the Middle East, dependence on foreign oil, and chemical warfare. It's one of the enduring strengths of the country that the average guy at the corner store believes he has some small influence, and some great responsibility.

"That Iraq fella is going to get what's coming to him," said the man waiting in the barbershop to get his short hair cut shorter. "That's my prediction."

There's something for everyone here. The word "Vietnam,"

which keeps cropping up in discussions about troop strength and the American involvement, speaks to the collective memory of one generation of Americans. The word "Hitler," which has been used profligately in discussions of the Iraqi leader, speaks to another. (The public-opinion mavens who've been asking people how Hussein compares with Hitler should be prosecuted for carrying a loaded question.) The angle for kids: Saddam Hussein is Bart Simpson cubed. Bad attitude, dude.

Life goes on, but not on its usual track. Even the president couldn't keep up the illusion of normalcy. He vacates well, but he has to watch appearances. People still remember that he went hunting at the tail end of the Panama invasion.

He told the rest of us to go on with our lives, and then instead of staying put in Kennebunkport, with the phone in his golf cart and his cigarette boat, he took a short trip back to Washington. It was a Daddy vacation. A couple of days in a business suit, a couple of days in a vest with lots of little pockets and hooks and feathers all over it. Takes me back.

This all takes me back. Gas shortages, double-digit inflation, trouble in the Middle East—these are the things that shaped my formative years. I thought someday we'd gather around the Weber kettle and pass them along to our children in stories and song. Now they're experiencing them firsthand. All they hear about is the Middle East, and Lyme disease. "Are we having a war?" one asked, and in the fashion of my times, I answered, "Sort of." Then we toss a Frisbee around, and wait to hear the news from around the world at the roadside produce stand.

SUMMER'S
SOLDIERS

September 13, 1990

At the county fair the armored personnel carrier stood between the pony rides and the dart game. Boys passed through it all afternoon, poring over the controls, running their hands along its camouflage-colored body. "It is not a tank," said a soldier sternly each time a boy raised on G.I. Joe mislabeled the thing. It seemed to fall somewhere between a Trans Am and the Tilt-A-Whirl in the minds of the kids, to have as much to do with death as the John Deere tractor exhibit.

Soldiers go to war, and sometimes they kill and die. We all know this. And yet, in some peculiar sense, it slipped our minds. In the last fifteen years, we have slowly lost our perception of the Army, the Air Force, the Navy, and the Marines as groups whose primary goal is to defend our country. The peacetime armed forces have become the largest vocational training school in the nation.

The average age of a new recruit this year was twenty, and many of them joined up for reasons that had nothing to do with combat, or even with patriotism. The stories take on a kind of Main Street sameness. dissatisfaction with a dead-end job, in a factory, a fast-food restaurant, a small office. Enlisting has become part of a great American postadolescence for some men and women not smart, not rich, or not directed enough for college. Looking to learn computers or communications, attracted by tuition grants, egged on by parents, they signed up.

The military knows this. Its appeals now have little to do with patriotism, no stern Uncle Sam with an I WANT YOU! above his inexorable index finger. They speak largely to self-interest, a kind of yuppie armed forces.

There's a moment in the movie *Private Benjamin*, about a spoiled rich girl who becomes a better person in boot camp. "Excuse me," she says to a sergeant, "but I think they sent me to the wrong place. You see, I did join the Army, but I joined a different Army. I joined the one with the condos and the private rooms."

Last week in the same magazines that carried accounts of troop deployments, there were recruitment ads for women. "If you're looking for an experience that could help you get an edge on life and be a success," the ads say. They even suggest that the Army is a good place to meet guys, which I have to assume is correct.

Can the families of our soldiers be blamed if the events of the last month have left them dazed and confused? Can a father who wrote an opinion piece saying that he will not forgive the president if his son is killed in Saudi Arabia, who wrote of his son's companions that "they joined the Marines as a way of earning enough money to go to college" really be blamed for his blind spot? Can a nineteen-year-old woman saying good-bye to her baby son who tells *People* magazine, "I never thought of anything like this when I joined up," really be blamed for a statement that sounds so painfully naive?

Can grandparents who find it incredible that any employer would send both parents of young children simultaneously on a long and dangerous business trip be blamed for their distress? Those who see the world in black and white reply that the military is not just any employer. But that is precisely how it has positioned itself in recent memory.

It's not just a job, it's an adventure.

There is a schizophrenic quality to American feeling about this military action in almost every quote you read from average people. On the one hand, they say that we should be there, making short work of Saddam Hussein. On the other hand, they say they want no American lives lost.

Some of this is the natural sentiment surrounding war, and some is skepticism over our reasons for being in the Persian Gulf in the first place. But some is occasioned by modern military recruitment, recruitment that, under current circumstances, smacks of deceptive advertising. In times of conscription no soldier's mother could fool herself about his ultimate purpose. We always knew that purpose was still there, but somehow it slipped our minds, the fact that "Be all that you can be" could be transformed into "to be or not to be" overnight.

Ever since the United States sent troops to the Middle East, American citizens have publicly yearned for decisive victory without bloodshed—that is, war without war. It would be nice to think that this reflects faith in the power of diplomacy, but it would not be entirely true. Thousands of American homes were unprepared for this eventuality. Thousands of parents sent their twenty-year-olds away to learn a trade. Now they find that they really sent them into battle. And I cannot blame them if some of them find that unreal, or even unfair.

NEW WORLD AT WAR

November 15, 1990

When the police arrived they found the three children alone. They were wearing dirty clothes because they hadn't figured out how to do the laundry, and their father had tacked a note to the wall, telling them how to get cash with his automatic teller card. They were eight, twelve, and thirteen, and they were hungry. There was no food in the house. Their father had been gone a week.

He'd left for the Persian Gulf.

The case of Staff Sergeant Faagalo Savaiki is a worst-case scenario, an extreme illustration of the collision between a changing American way of life and the demands of war. He is divorced, his ex-wife lives in Hawaii, and she couldn't manage to pay the airfare to Tennessee, which is where the children were living with their father. He's back in the States now, charged with child abuse; the children are in foster homes, and the 101st Airborne Division, to which Sergeant Savaiki belongs, is still in the Middle East.

The world has changed since this country was last at war. It's not simply the shifting sands of geopolitics. In the waning years of Vietnam we were approaching our two hundredth birthday, an adolescent country still devoted to muscling any comers aside and being the undisputed champion of the world. We've grown up since. And there is nothing quite so sobering as becoming adult and discovering the real world.

The if of war in the Middle East has turned in many of our minds to a when. We know that once upon a time there were formal declarations of such developments, but that seems so idealistic now. We remember, too, that once we believed we fought wars for reasons straight from the side of some marble monument. We are realistic about this conflict as only a grown-up, slightly world-weary country can be. We are going to war for oil, and, by extension, for the economy. The president trots out his Hitler similes to try to convince us otherwise.

The military is as changed as the rest of us. A support group in California reports that many of the soldiers writing home ask about public opinion, about whether we're for them or against them. They remember Vietnam; they know that uncomplicated patriotism is no longer our style. Eleven percent of our armed forces personnel are female today, more than a tenfold increase over twenty years ago. If heavy fighting begins, a significant number of casualties will be women. People who yearn for the good old days are sure that women in body bags will convince us that women have overstepped their bounds.

For those of us who believe sons are as precious as daughters, it will simply provide further illustration that war is hell.

There are still plenty of military families with a *The Best Years of Our Lives* quality, the mother waiting with the children for Daddy to come home from the Gulf. But the number of single parents in America has doubled in the last twenty years, and 55,000 of them are in the service, along with an undetermined number of two-soldier couples. When they joined up, they were told that they had to assign guardianship for their children; there is no blanket combat exemption in an all-volunteer army for someone with babies to care for or someone raising children alone.

Most have found temporary homes for their children with relatives. But at least two mothers ordered to the Mideast have left the Army, one because her children would not stop fighting with the cousins with whom they were bunking, and another because her parents became too ill to care for her baby daughter. Both women are fighting to be given honorable discharges.

The military is providing more counseling for its families than ever before. The relatives left at home, from Staten Island to Seattle, are tying yellow ribbons around trees and telephone poles. This will be a different war, in some ways, than any we have fought before, because this is a different kind of country. Our reality has outstripped the traditional stories of brave men going out to fight and die for a great cause while their women wait staunchly at home and provide security and normalcy for the children.

We have become more complicated than the scripts of old movies. Now we have brave women going out to fight and die for a cause none of us are sure about while their children struggle to feel secure with grandparents or aunts or uncles. Or a father who instructs the children in how to use his bank card and then leaves for Saudi Arabia. There is neither the kind of acceptance that lulled many of us at the beginning of Vietnam, nor the rage and betrayal that lit up the end. There is a quiet disillusionment: Ah, this again. And for what?

THE QUESTIONS
CONTINUE

November 25, 1990

It's hard to imagine that there was an American household this Thanksgiving that did not have at its holiday table a liberal helping of war talk laced with confusion, skepticism, and doubt.

Even in Dhahran, a truckload of soldiers driving past a group of reporters opened fire, armed with loaded questions. "I want to go home!" two of them shouted. "This isn't our war! What are we doing here? Why are we over here? We aren't supposed to be here—this isn't our war!"

It's hard to know if the president is really listening to questions like those, shouted out by two young men who may die for his decision. The threat of war sends presidents into a dizzying spiral of self-justification; George Bush could soon become as isolated from real public opinion as Lyndon Johnson became in the shadow of his war and as Richard Nixon's war kept him insulated from beginning to end.

Many of the questions have been inspired by the president's public fumbling for the right answers. First we were defending the sovereignty of little Kuwait. Then we were repelling Saddam Hussein, the new Hitler. (This appears to be the standard by which all foes will herein be judged; whether they are properly Hitlerian or not. Madmen too; they must be madmen.) When these reasons proved too broad, we segued to oil and jobs. The president made a package of all, combined them with the impending threat of Iraq's nuclear capability and offered this to the troops on Thanksgiving Day.

Vietnam hangs like Marley's ghost over these holiday celebrations, ready to provide us with the present and future contained in the past. For the president, this is as much a millstone around his neck as all the chains and cashboxes were around Marley's. But I wish he could be taken by spirits, as Scrooge was, into taverns and kitchens and city streets to hear public opinion that is not handpicked or filtered through the screen of advisers or reporters, to know the consumers of his foreign policy.

What he would see are Americans talking, talking, talking. Arguing. Anguishing. Wondering. Wishing. Remembering past mistakes and vowing not to repeat them. We will not blame the troops this time for doing the politician's business; we know it is possible to support the soldiers and repudiate the policies. And we will talk about the politician's business as our own—before, not after.

We know from experience that the reasons to sacrifice our children's lives must be clear and compelling. The economic consequences of a stranglehold on oil are the most tangible but the least effective rationale for this war. If the president knows the American people at all, he certainly knows one thing: they never have been and never will be people who will knowingly trade their sons and daughters for economic stability.

The president left Saudi Arabia still trailing more questions than answers: if we are going to war to counter the threat of atomic weapons in the hands of a madman, does that make us the nuclear policeman of the world, ready to step in whenever some despot becomes technologically sophisticated and border-oblivious? Can we live as a country with the knowledge that once again the children of the poor and of people of color will be killed for the convictions of well-to-do white men? And how much of the decision to go into combat will be reasonable, how much the president's subconscious fear of the wimp factor that has dogged him, and has always dogged our feisty nation? Will this be a war built, on both sides, around that thankless business of saving face?

George Bush tries often to be consumer-responsive. Critics think this makes him unprincipled, and admirers believe it means he's pragmatic. It is a problem when he misreads the consumer.

Because he thought baby boomers were looking for the same thing in a running mate that they wanted in a sports car—recent vintage, good looks—he impulsively chose Dan Quayle. He overlooked the value Americans place on intelligence and experience. He cannot act impulsively again. He cannot overlook how smart and experienced the consumers are.

"What are we doing here?" the soldiers in the truck shouted. And there are millions more like them here at home. Traditionally, a war begins and public opinion follows. And that opinion is bolstered by patriotism and loyalty, the feeling that American soldiers dying thousands of miles away deserve our unquestioning support at home. It's happened backward this time. We are envisioning the body bags, and that is a very, very good thing: If the president thinks a declaration of war would mute the questions of the people, he has misread his consumers.

IN THE SHADOW
OF WAR

January 13, 1991

On the imitation-wood-grain surface of the table lay a pile of fliers, small print dominated by letters two inches high: STOP THE WAR NOW! Like Proust's madeleine, it flung me back, to hundreds of undergraduate bulletin boards, dozens of speeches, but especially to one march in 1972. I held my notebook like a shield between my face and the angry man, on his way home from the night shift, who was watching people move down the avenue beneath banners of peace. "Put down that they're disgrace to this country," he shouted over the noise of the chanting "Put down that I'm a veteran of World War II."

By the imitation-wood-grain table sat a man, narrow as an exclamation point, telling why he came to the first meeting of the New York City chapter of the Military Families Support Network. "I'm a World War II veteran," he said softly. "My youngest son is in the Gulf. I keep thinking there's going to be a war. There must be another way of dealing with this. It seems to be going on every twenty years. It has to stop."

Today we wake in the shadow of war, some from the sound sleep of onlookers, others from the long restless nights of parents, wives, husbands, and children of soldiers. The antiwar effort now is immediate and powerful, as though it were a kind of retribution. This time, the activists seem to be saying, we will get it right. There are marches and vigils planned aplenty. There is an 800 number that provides information on resistance and a 900 number that arranges overnight delivery of letters to senators and congressmen. Nearly every leading religious denomination and several powerful labor unions have come out in opposition to war in the Persian Gulf.

This is not because of great similarities between Southeast Asia and the Middle East. It is because of great differences between who we are now and who we were then. With the end of the Cold War, the bust of our economic boom, and the disintegration of our families, we are a nation struggling to understand itself. One of the most powerful events of our national history was fermenting and souring twenty years ago, a war that divided and defined us in ways we came to hate.

Our national character has changed. Our notions of masculinity, always linked to our notions of face and force, are different today. The woman thing, as the president might call it, has shaped this development. Statistics show a gender gap: 57 percent of men in a recent *Times* poll favored military action if Iraq does not withdraw from Kuwait by Tuesday's deadline, while 37 percent said we should give sanctions more time to work. The results for women were almost exactly the opposite: 36 percent voted for immediate action, 56 percent for patience. Our earliest image of this conflict was of women in camouflage fatigue kissing their children good-bye; say what we will about the idea that fathers are as important as mothers, it made some people think on a more human scale about what war means. (Memo to Senator Alfonse D'Amato: Forget the rhetoric about "our boys" during debates and fast-forward to 1991.) Last week a group of feminists demonstrated, personifying the button making the rounds: WE'RE GOING TO WAR TO DEFEND PEOPLE WHO WON'T LET WOMEN DRIVE?

To the extent that we still think of men as resolving differences through force and women through talk, there is a feminization of national feeling. Macho is no longer our national pastime, and there seems to be a declining number of little boys exhorted to "go out there and fight like a man." So far, there have been no "Love It or Leave It" bumper stickers. "I love my country, but . . ." began two of the testimonials at the Military Families Support Network meeting.

We no longer have illusions about war. We have seen the carnage on CNN. Some protesters are sending the White House black plastic trash bags, to remind the president of how people come home from combat. The shadow that hangs over us all seems to be the shadow of another war. But it is really the shadow of what we will think of ourselves when this is over. Dorothy Thompson, for many years America's most prominent woman columnist, wrote a column after World War II about disarmament. "You cannot talk to the mothers with planes and atomic bombs," she wrote. "You must come into the room of your mother unarmed."

Some of her editors found her sentiments treacly and hard to take. Those sentiments need to be updated in one respect: many of the fathers now feel the same way. Some people consider this a failure of will. I think it's progress.

PERSONALLY

January 17, 1991

Woman walks into a bakery, where there's a sign announcing that the price of bagels will go up a nickel on January 15. "War and an increase in the price of bagels on the same day," she says.

"I hope he backs down," says the baker.

"Who?" says the woman. "Saddam Hussein or George Bush?"

"Either one," the baker says.

Bagels were more expensive yesterday, and war broke out. Real life was peculiar, with an edge of sadness and of slow motion, and a sense of New Year's Eve gone nuclear: only one shopping day till Armageddon. "Now it is our job to shift without too much awkwardness ..." Bob Costas said Saturday on *NBC Sports*, segueing from reports of the Gulf War to a football postmortem. That is what it is like. Dinner and war. Homework and war. The mundane and the horrible.

There's a moment in one of the *Godfather* movies when a capo is being executed for disloyalty. "It was business," he says of his traitorous behavior.

This is personal.

It's personal for Saddam Hussein. This war is a career move. His psyche has been dissected like a biology-class frog, but it seems to me that he suffers from a lethal dose of egomania, that craziness that affects anyone audacious enough to lead a nation. The secretary general of the United Nations came to call, hoping to avert the deaths of thousands upon thousands of people, and when he left Saddam Hussein delivered this non sequitur: "He met the American president four times before coming to us."

This brings to mind the moment in Woody Allen's *Bananas* when the new dictator of a Central American country belittles the danish Mr. Allen has brought him. "He brings cake for a group of people," complains one of the dictator's aides, "he doesn't even bring an assortment." Saddam Hussein's comment might be humorous in its egocentricity if it were not so ominous, such a clear indication of how he has intertwined this conflict with those two little words, Big Man.

For George Bush this is personal, too. I don't think the wimp factor is the only thing at work here. But I think that the sled of public positioning always stands at the top of a slippery slope, and when it begins to move, it is difficult to stop it or slow it down, even when half the electorate are yelling, "Wait a minute!" Sanctions needed more time to work, more time than the sled allowed. But that, alas, is yesterday's story.

This is personal. Most people agree that Saddam Hussein is pond scum and that he can't be permitted to take Kuwait as though it were the lunch money of the littlest kid in class. But then they ask themselves this question: Would I sacrifice my child for this?

And the answer is no.

I only hope that we will continue, when this is done, to take these issues personally. We should take personally the fact that we habitually give aid to the kind of men we can easily and accurately describe as monsters.

We should take personally the fact that few politicians have had the guts or the vision to shape a coherent energy policy that would lessen our dependence on foreign oil. And we should take personal responsibility for the fact that we have not had the will to conserve or change.

We should take personally the idea that if there is to be a new world order, it must include a new answer to the question: Why us? It is time for our messiah complex to get a good overhaul. We can no longer afford economically, psychologically, or politically to be the policeman of the world, even if we are the first one called when someone needs a cop.

That will be then. This is now. Time has stopped. So do our hearts, each time a clinch on *One Life to Live* is punctuated by the words "We interrupt this program to bring you a special report. . . ." In Des Moines, a teenager demonstrating against the war said he did not want a big black wall in Washington with his name on it. In the desert, a soldier wrote to his wife saying that he would understand if she remarried. It came to me that no matter how swift the conflict, we will someday soon be reading about the design for the memorial to its dead.

"When do they decide to call it World War III?" a friend asked the other day.

I don't know. There's so much we don't know today. I only know that everyone seems sad and afraid, that the loss and mourning began even before the fighting. We are taking this very personally indeed.

THE BACK FENCE

January 20, 1991

If anyone had looked inside the meeting room, they would have seen a peculiar sight. More than a hundred people had paid to hear a lecture, but the speaker had stepped aside because of certain circumstances and instead the audience was staring at a kind of Frankenstein monster, a figure with a brown podium for a body and a small television for a head. Suddenly the head had a face, the face of George Bush, telling the nation it had gone to war.

We had always expected it to be the television war, and that is what it has been. Tom and Dan and Peter and the pleasant generic newsreaders of Cable News Network stared into our eyes day after day, night after night. No one could bear to turn them off.

But it is not the television war we expected. There has been precious little war to see in these first few days: magnificent planes, the occasional soldier, a few minutes of footage of what looked like a fireworks display shot in bad light. And the talking heads: this has been a great windfall for retired generals. Once we learned that war had actually begun and Israel had been hit, there was little to discover except that Peter Jennings looks fresh as a daisy on a few hours' sleep.

It was not because of the press of news that we seemed incapable of turning the TV off. The television had become a kind of modern communal meeting place from which to absorb history aborning. It was America's back fence, the one place in this time of dislocation where we were all connected, all having the same sensation at the same time, even if the sensation was shame at thinking that a correspondent in a gas mask looked like a mutant bug.

The television war, they called Vietnam, and it was because it taught us what it really looked like, what happens before the clutch of soldiers hoists the flag to the top of the hill. It made real all the ugly stuff, the brutality and the blood. Red is the color of war. Mr. Jennings recalled the other day that General Westmoreland once complained in those days that the television camera saw such a narrow view. But it was wide enough.

The television hasn't had a view for these last few days; in truth, television has acted like radio, with still photographs of faces superimposed on maps. But action was not all we were looking for. Sitting in front of the television was the closest we could come to compartmentalizing the sea change. The most enduring memory of my childhood is of a time much like this one, those long November days of watching the Kennedy murder, the mourning and the burial, in the blackest blacks and the whitest whites I have ever known. Before this, that was the most continuous television I had ever watched. Like this, it did not provide much news. It gave you a feeling of America sitting in a circle.

What Americans have seen these last few days is what they had hoped and prayed for: war without tears. The descriptions of how this missile was picking off that one sounded like a grand video game of the sky. Fighting raged for three days, and the closest we came to seeing casualties was a crumpled van on a Tel Aviv street.

Everyone hoped that was because things were going well, whatever that means. Or perhaps it is because no one really knows exactly how things are going. Reporters are far away from the front, reporting from hotel rooms with sealed windows or basements where they crouch for safety's sake. The Department of Defense is taking pool reporters where it wants them to go, which is nowhere much.

So for now, we are eased into the unspeakable, confronting the concept of combat well before we confront its realities, an incremental process that can only benefit those who believe this is a noble endeavor. We see map war, diagram war, computer war. The closest anyone got to something else was CNN, which has given new meaning to the term "intelligence network." For half a day it had three reporters in a Baghdad hotel room describing bombs bursting in air. But the Iraqis cut off their communications, perhaps because Dick Cheney said at a televised briefing that he was getting information from their dispatches. A television war, indeed. The Iraqis watch the Secretary of Defense on television reporting that he is monitoring the front by watching television.

A new age has begun. Our children will date themselves by the grade they were in when the United States fought Iraq. And as soon as we get accustomed to that, we will need more than retired generals. What we have seen in these first few days is a kind of primitive ritual made modern. When things are very scary, we are afraid to be alone in the dark. There have been people and light in our living rooms. Don't confuse that with war or news. Both are yet to come.

THE DOMESTIC
FRONT

There are many ways to watch America in action, but one of the most colorful is to stroll the public spaces of the Port Authority Bus Terminal, that squat, ever-busy gateway to the world on wheels. You can learn something about the State of the Union by the state of this place. And it has precious little to do with cuts in the capital-gains tax.

The irony of the terminal is that the building has never looked better, with neon wall sculptures and bright lighting. It's the people that are the problem. The scamsters, who do a booming business in selling telephone calling card numbers for ten dollars a shot. The runaways, their eyes as old as the stories they can tell about serial parents, prepubescent incest, and foster homes. The broken men, with years of booze running red in the veins of their faces. "Excuse me, sweetheart," some of them say as you edge past, proving that chivalry is not dead, it's just drunk.

And all around them move the commuters, angry at being

panhandled, tired of walking over prone bodies to get to the greener, cleaner places where they live.

America is a little like this now. In some ways it has never looked better, with its flags flying and the yellow ribbons tied around its trees. It's the inside that's rotting away, the domestic disintegration that war has given us all an excuse to forget.

On television, reports said that children in Israel were sleeping in hotels, homeless because of the war. Children in New York slept in hotels for years because they were homeless.

On television they showed bombed buildings that were shells amid fields of rubble. I've seen those broken buildings and rubble fields in forgotten neighborhoods all over New York.

The same country that has rallied round pushing Iraq out of Kuwait has given up on parts of itself. Infant mortality. Teenage pregnancy. Drugs. Dropouts. Bank failures. Home foreclosures. We walk around the bad stuff on our way to somewhere else and mutter under our breath: "Own fault, own fault."

Fault is not the point. A capable, no-nonsense woman named Janis Beitzer runs the little world of the bus terminal, and it would be perfectly understandable if she said her job was to put people on buses and all the rest is someone else's problem. But that would be shortsighted, like missing the opportunity to rally people united behind a war abroad around an equally horrible war at home. Rerouting traffic patterns to discourage loitering, opening a drop-in center for the homeless, hiring social service workers—she's had to deal with issues no one running a bus terminal ever had to consider before.

"We didn't really have a choice," Ms. Beitzer says.

Neither do we. America often has a one-track mind, and the track in the last month has led straight to the Persian Gulf. The president knew where the ovations lay in his State of the Union address, a kind of boilerplate noble-cause speech that could have been delivered by any American president engaged in battle abroad. When he praised the men and women fighting in the Gulf, a great roar went up from his audience.

But the domestic initiatives in his speech were sketchy, per-functory, and shockingly beside the point. At a time when many Americans still believe this war is inextricably linked to our reliance on foreign oil, he kissed off energy conservation with one vague sentence. Elimination of PACs and a cut in capital-gains taxes don't seem like pressing issues for a country with thousands of people sleeping in the streets and thousands of mothers giving birth to addicted babies.

Time magazine named George Bush "Men of the Year" at the beginning of the month, declaring him adept at foreign affairs and fuzzy on domestic issues. It was the first known case of a multiple-personality defense for an elected official. Now the president has a mandate to play to his strengths and to forget the national weaknesses. And his own.

A one-track mind is not enough for government. If the president thinks only of war, the home front will have disintegrated, in some cases beyond repair.

The soldiers he invoked to such rousing effect the other night will come home. Some of them will lose their houses if the reces-sion continues. Some of them will watch their children die on city streets if we do not do something about crime and drugs. Some of them might even wind up someday in a bus terminal, sleeping on the floor, in the home of the free and the brave. When that happens we will know that we have lost the war, the war we turned our backs on while we were busy with yellow rib-bons.

February 7, 1991

It's often used as a sour quip, the sentence "Hindsight is always twenty-twenty," a dismissive remark, a coda. But then you see hindsight with tears in its eyes, and realize that perhaps this is one of our greatest tragedies, that our mistakes become clear to us only when we see them over our shoulders, trailing us like an ugly dog.

Hindsight is 20-20 for Robert McNamara, the secretary of defense who raised the Vietnam War from its childhood through its horrid years as an uncontrollable early adolescent. Hindsight is 20-20 for Lee Atwater, the twangy campaign whiz who never met a clever, nasty remark he didn't like and who helped make George Bush palatable, and president.

Both men are troubled by their pasts, which would be only terribly sad if it were not that their pasts are our history. Because of that, their torment is a national tragedy, and their regrets prefigure our future.

Mr. Atwater writes in the current issue of *Life* magazine about the days since he discovered that he had a malignant brain tumor. The pictures are heartbreaking. Somewhere inside the bloated, limp body in bed and wheelchair is the sassy guitar player who celebrated the 1988 Republican victory by throwing a blues concert. But you can't see him here.

He talks about the triumphs, but what it all comes down to is this: that he has found God and discovered the sheer meanness of his professional style. "In 1988," he says, "fighting Dukakis, I said that I 'would strip the bark off the little bastard' and 'make Willie Horton his running mate.' I am sorry for both statements: the first for its naked cruelty, the second because it makes me sound racist, which I am not."

Mr. McNamara appears in *Time*, talking to Carl Bernstein, and his words make you want to weep, for him and for our bungled opportunities. Of Vietnam he says, "because of misinformation and misperceptions, there are misjudgments as to where a nation's interests lie and what can be accomplished." It is a statement with great resonance these days. Of the exaggeration of the Communist threat he concludes, "We could have maintained deterrence with a fraction of the number of warheads we built."

The regrets of two men, one aging, the other dying. Mr. Atwater helped poison the level of electoral discourse, so that those two words may never seem seemly in tandem again. Mr. McNamara was a primary architect of the war that cost this country thousands of young lives and its illusions about itself. In different ways, at different times, they contributed to the notion that we are a nation of bullies.

Can George Bush's second thoughts on the war in the Persian Gulf be many decades behind?

It reminds me of fathers who come to their children, now grown, and say, "These are the mistakes I made. Please forgive me." And we do forgive, but we are saddled with our characters, shaped by those mistakes.

It reminds me of what that graceful writer Paul Fussell, who is at work on an anthology of writings about war, once said, "If we do not redefine manhood, war is inevitable."

And Mr. Atwater's words about one of his daughters, pretending to interview him: "She had seen me interviewed so many times on TV, perhaps she thought that was the only way she could find out the truth. Watching her, I felt guilty about the degree to which my career—and my illness—have robbed me of crucial time with my children."

And Mr. McNamara, who says that his wife's death may have been hastened by the national trauma of Vietnam—"She was with me on occasions when people said I had blood on my hands"—and who is asked by Mr. Bernstein about the people who really know him, the real McNamara, the inner man. Here is the answer: "People don't know, and probably not my kids. And let me tell you that's a weakness. If you're not known emotionally to people, it means you haven't really communicated fully to people. I know it's a weakness of mine. But I'm not about to change now."

We're not about to change now. Manhood stands with its old definitions: aggression, winning at all costs, work over family, control over vulnerability. And, finally, regrets as corrosive as Mr. Atwater's disease, as sad as Mr. McNamara's eyes—about what we did in the world, about who we are at home, two things that are inseparable.

War was inevitable. And inevitable, too, someday, will be the hindsight, the documents that tell us this was unnecessary and ill advised, the advisers who reveal their misgivings years too late. The regrets, in hindsight.

RESERVATIONS NOT ACCEPTED

February 24, 1991

The group of veterans marched down the street, and as they came into sight the crowd at the curb seemed to move forward to greet them, to hold them like a hug. They were youngish men, and their camouflage clothes were as different from the neat uniforms of the other groups as their war had been from other wars. Beside me an old man waved a flag. "We're with you," he shouted, as though he were putting all our cheers into words, and then he added, "We should have let you finish what you started." And the smile froze on my face, and fell.

It was five years ago that those Vietnam veterans marched by on Memorial Day, but I've thought about that scene more than once in the last forty days. From the beginning, it has been difficult to publicly oppose this war, to express reservations or even to forgo the exuberant displays of national accord.

A basketball player at Seton Hall University who did not wear a flag patch on his uniform was heckled so relentlessly by fans that he quit the team and the school. The editor of *The Kutztown* (PA)

Patriot was fired, and while the owners said there were other reasons, the ax fell just after he ran an antiwar editorial with the
headline "How About a Little PEACE!"—the last word in letters
as big as your finger. What amazed him afterward, he said, were
the people who called him eager to talk geopolitics, as though
they were all members of a sub-rosa self-help group: Hi. My name
is Joe, and I have reservations about the war in the Gulf.

Reservations are not accepted. There were antiwar demonstrations. But mostly there was the majority rallying around the president, and a silent minority, constrained by the atmosphere of
high-octane Amerimania, a prettified second cousin of her "Love
It or Leave It" forebears. Some of us were ambivalent, but we
don't do ambivalence well in America. We do courage of our convictions. We do might makes right. Ambivalence is French. Certainty is American.

Some people say dissent is a matter of time, that opposition to
Vietnam took years to build. But I believe it's a sign of the times
instead. America had become the Muhammad Ali of nations, bat-
tered by foreign competition, by a faltering economy, by domestic problems as big as our national ambition. In the last six
months Americans saw themselves as the leaders of the world
again, assured of their inherent greatness and the essential evil of
the enemy.

But the line between such convictions and jingoism can be
very thin. Everyone talked about standing behind the soldiers
even while deploring the policy. "Support the troops—bring
them home alive," one protest sign read. But, like my neighbor at
the parade, Letters to the Editor columns in dozens of newspapers made clear that people believed the way to show support was
to agree that the troops were engaged in a necessary and a noble
enterprise. If not, keep quiet. The idea that our true greatness
lies in our diversity and freedom of speech was, if anything, a P.S.

This war has taken on a momentum of its own. The troops of
August led to the buildup of autumn, and that to the combat of
January 16. The cumulative effect was epitomized at a rally in

California several weeks ago: as though they were in the bleach-
ers, a bunch of boys were chanting, "We're Number One!"

When the Soviet Union stepped in as a deal maker, our former
dark star, our one-time evil twin, it was hard to bear, especially
when the negotiations included Saddam Hussein's survival. His
face has been plastered on dart boards and Ping-Pong paddles,
and his mustache has become an instant metaphor for evil. The
U.N. resolutions called for making him leave Kuwait. The grass-
roots agenda, forged over heady days of the United States leading the world to war, is to destroy him. It is an agenda that lends
itself to ultimatums, not negotiations.

"We should have let you finish what you started," I keep hearing that man yelling. Some of us believed that our national
agenda in the Gulf War was murky from the start. But it has
grown even clearer: we must win, and Saddam Hussein must lose.
Trouble is, it's not that kind of world, and this isn't that kind of
war. Saddam Hussein could lose big and still be a hero in some
parts of the region. We could run a devastating military campaign and still wind up hated and reviled. But for some short
time, the war in the Persian Gulf has made the world a simpler
place. Black and white. Good and bad. Win and lose. But not for
long.

THE MICROWAVE WAR

March 3, 1991

Barely eighteen hours after the war ended, a man was on Broadway near Times Square hawking victory T-shirts. WE WON! they said on the front, the words flanked by two American flags— OPERATION DESERT STORM. JAN. 16—FEB. 27. All I could think of was some smooth small-time entrepreneur, standing with one eye on the television and one on the boys in the back room, yelling "Roll 'em, Harry" at the moment that the president said, "I am pleased to announce that at midnight tonight. . . ." This is some amazing country, where you can turn a commemorative item around in less than a day.

It was like that from beginning to end, the microwave war, ready to be consumed, digested, and cleared away in a fraction of the usual time. No wonder the television people seemed to be running on 78 rpm for the first week. The ground war took less time than it takes to get over the flu. And fewer Americans died in combat over the six weeks of the Gulf War than are habitually murdered in New York City during a comparable period of time.

To read over the early predictions is an exercise in the fallibility of political scientists, retired military men, pundits, politicians, and the press. The war on the ground would be long. It would be bloody. The Iraqi Army would use chemical weapons. Their numbers were great. They were relentless. It all seems like a parody now.

Throughout this brief and enormous encounter, I kept remembering a peacenik line from my past: What if they gave a war and nobody came? The enemy never really showed up. When we were in the air, we supposed he was saving his knockout punch for the ground. Instead, on the ground, he marched beneath a flag of white. We talked at home about not automatically associating the troops with the policy. It turned out the troops not in tune with their policy were the ones on the other side.

Euphoria has been one of the war's buzzwords. We have been repeatedly cautioned not to feel it. The president said the other night this was not the time for it. It has never crossed my mind. I am reasonably sure of only three things today: that George Bush will be reelected president in 1992; that if he chose either Colin Powell or Norman Schwarzkopf as his running mate, he might win by the largest landslide in the history of the nation; and that we are incredibly skilled at war.

I know that the last should provide a certain security. When I was trying to feel something the night the peace began, something more electric than fatigue and relief, I pictured all the homes in which people must be holding one another and grinning with wet faces because someone who meant the whole world to them was alive and whole and coming home. There were many more of those scenes that night than we ever expected when we talked about thousands of casualties, when we wondered how many lives were too many.

The lesson we learned from Vietnam was that it was possible for the United States to be an abject failure in the theater of war. The lesson we've learned from this is that we are a smashing success. Because of technology and tactics and training, we are a staggering fighting force.

We have learned that we do this superlatively. And that frightens me.

Oh, if it makes each nation in the world think thrice about aggression because it fears the biggest kid in class, I say hooray. But if it makes us cocky—and a cocky American is the cockiest creature on earth—that will be a disaster. The failure of Vietnam made us gun-shy for almost two decades. It is a much greater failure to be trigger-happy. If the Iraqi rout becomes our model of conflict resolution, we will have suffered a great defeat.

Too soon to tell. That is our refrain. Never has the first rough draft of history been produced under such deadline pressure.

Not far from the T-shirt stand was that spot on Times Square where people celebrated the end of World War II, and where a photographer took that picture of a soldier kissing a woman, with the celebration raging around them, that is one of our great visual images of the euphoria that can accompany victory and peace. Perhaps we will see images like that when the soldiers come home.

The test may be the T-shirt, twenty years from now, a relic at the bottom of someone's dresser drawer, a reminder of the last time we went to war. "Every twenty years it happens," a soldier's father said to me when this all began, all those years ago, in January. Maybe now we have the authority, and the confidence, to allow that span to stretch. This is the peace before the storm. Now comes the testing of our mettle.

NO THERE THERE

May 6, 1992

On a campaign trip to a South Carolina college campus twelve years ago, George Bush told his audience, "I'll be glad to reply to or dodge your questions, depending on what I think will help our election most."

At the time it was a throwaway line. In retrospect it sounds like something that should have been needlepointed on a pillow. Maybe that's unnecessary; the do-what-sells gene in George Bush's character seems so overdeveloped as to be ineradicable.

Last week, watching the president on the first day after the Rodney King verdict was like watching a man in sweatsocks negotiate a freshly waxed floor. Slip, slip, slide. Slip, slip, slide. He went from saying the jury system had worked to expressing shock at the verdict. You could picture him studying polls and modifying the stance.

He finally gave a neat little speech, a generic speech with no real sense of what the most powerful leader in our nation was thinking and feeling at one of the most powerful moments in recent history. Instead of reaching deep inside himself for some anecdote about his own feelings on racism, he had a generic tale of black samaritans superimposed on a law-and-order riff. He announced a federal investigation. He called up the Guard. He committed money.

That is government.

The difference between government and leadership is that leadership has a soul.

Supporters of Governor Bill Clinton have asked over and over when those of us who crank out copy are going to bring character questions to bear upon George Bush. And by that they seem to mean questions about the president's personal life or about his son's business dealings.

But the truth is there is an enormous character issue here. The problem is that it is not true/false or multiple choice. It is an essay question.

What does Mr. Bush stand for?

His old friend C. Fred Chambers, an oil-company executive, once said, "George understands that you have to do politically prudent things to get in a position to do what you want." Problem is, Mr. Bush has been in position for three years and we still don't know what he wants to do other than be politically prudent for seven more months so he can win reelection. It is the opposite of the emperor's new clothes. There are clothes, all right, depending on the prevailing winds, but nothing inside the empty suit.

Mr. Bush couldn't bring his great personal passions and ruling principles about race to bear on this crisis because he has none. Early this year *The New York Review of Books* ran a history of Mr. Bush's stands on civil rights issues that is a kind of road map of political expediency, from leading a campus drive at Yale for the United Negro College Fund in 1948 to campaigning for the Senate in Texas in 1964 by opposing the Civil Rights Act, to embracing a 1970 plan that advocated goals and timetables for hiring and promoting minorities, what the president today denigrates as quotas.

In fact he has done this on many of the great issues of our time. From the day in 1980 when the New York State Right to Life party said that his presence on the ticket ruled out an endorsement for Ronald Reagan to his position today as an anti-abortion ally—but not a champion, never a champion, champion is risky, champion is out there—Mr. Bush has slid from one politically convenient abortion stance to another.

My most enduring memories of the first Bush administration will be of a man needing principle and having only polls. He waffled on raising taxes. He went from being part of an administration that had propped up Saddam Hussein to dubbing Saddam a Hitler figure. He seemed at first flummoxed by how to react to the Soviet coup and then was halfhearted in his support for economic aid, as though even the traditional Red Menace philosophy was too rich for his blood.

Trollope, who created fictional politicians who were the mirror image of real ones, wrote in his autobiography that a successful politician "must be able to confine himself and confirm himself, to be satisfied with doing a little bit of a little thing at a time . . . If he have grand ideas, he must keep them to himself, unless by chance he can work his way up to the top of the tree." But by that time a fellow may have gotten out of the habits of grand ideas and nonconformity. There is a character issue for Mr. Bush in this campaign. The clothes have no emperor. There is no there there.

JUST SAY YES

April 1, 1992

Here's a suggested response for elected officials of a certain age when asked whether they smoked marijuana:

"Of course."

When political handlers are putting together position papers in the years to come, they should include an appendix they might as well call "The Rolling Papers." Exhibit A might be the way in which Governor Bill Clinton handled the dope issue when it came up this year. He backed, he filled, he clung to the letter of the question ("I have never broken the laws of my country"), and finally he said that, like so many other people of his generation, he did smoke marijuana when young, at Oxford when he was a Rhodes scholar. He then went on to explain.

Never explain.

One result was that Billy Crystal, who has made the Oscar telecast finally worth staying awake for, looked into the camera the other night and said, "Didn't inhale?" to a great guffaw from the audience. Mr. Clinton's suggestion that he smoked dope without inhaling made him look like either a fibber or a dork. Saying you smoked dope but didn't inhale is the equivalent of saying you drank beer but didn't swallow it.

I've been told that we're being particularly hard on Mr. Clinton this year, and I understand why some people are saying so. But they're missing the point. The point is that in some sense he's in the wrong place at the wrong time, running for president during a period of intense exploration of character issues. Like the rest of us, he's still not sure where the land mines lie, so he's wound up dancing around some questions best served by standing pat.

There are still purists who contend that character is not the point, that we should look solely at where candidates stand on the issues. That's foolish. We elect a whole person, not just a position paper on national health insurance or tax cuts. If George Bush loses in November, it will be for many reasons, but one will be that he just didn't seem like a real guy, who understood sad songs, shrunken paychecks, and macaroni meals.

Certainly the comely and charming Mr. Clinton, who promises to stick with us until the last dog dies, is running in part on his personality, and we've decided to explore it fully. We're still working out which culs-de-sac in the lives of candidates are dead ends and which teach us something important about the landscapes of their lives, which issues are character issues and which are peripheral ones. Sometimes we get it wrong. Ultimately the voters decide.

We assume that voters care about cheating, lying, lawbreaking. But we still don't really have a handle on whether people think infidelity counts as cheating or lying. And we have a pretty good idea that they're not much bothered by the breach of laws that accompanied smoking a joint. Character issues are changing things, peculiar to their time. It would be a ho-hum story today to uncover a candidate's short-lived first marriage when, just three decades ago, divorce was by way of disqualification. No one then talked much about sexual harassment; today it could torpedo a campaign.

Drug use has become ho-hum, too. The unwritten rule for public officials seems to be that they have to say they only did it once or twice and that they didn't enjoy it. For all of us who lived in dorm rooms with Indian-print bedspreads on the walls at around the same time they did, this seems not only foolish, but shortsighted.

One of the things that were so surreal about Nancy Reagan, in her trim little Adolfo suits, cruising the country to tell kids to just say no, was that she didn't have a clue as to why so many of them were saying yes. You could make an argument that those who have had a brush with drug use have some perspective on drug abuse. Instead of insisting that they didn't like it, why not admit that part of the allure of drugs is that they've been known to make you feel temporarily terrific? That's why people wind up using them to excess, particularly if they have lousy lives.

In the long shadow of crack and alcohol abuse, smoking marijuana has come to seem pretty tame. And it's apparent that soon it will be an anachronistic footnote in discussions of the character of the candidate. The drug issue has become insignificant as it has become unabashed. Short, sweet, without excuses or caveats: just say yes.

ADVANTAGE, MR. CLINTON

April 8, 1992

The daffodils are pressing skyward, the winter coats are ratty and in need of a good rest, and July will be here before we know it. It is time to get serious. We've enjoyed our season of none-of-the-above, the complaints that Mr. Right never stepped up to a podium and into our lives. Like the stages of serious illness, we've passed through anger and denial during this primary season. It is time for resolution, reconciliation, what the existential or the insurgent might call peace.

Bill Clinton is going to be the Democratic candidate for president.

And it's hard not to say that Mr. Clinton deserves it, impossible to think that a draft movement at the convention would be anything but grossly unfair. He has the experience; he's done the time. For a few more minutes we can entertain the notion of a composite candidate: the orator's gift of Cuomo, the war record of Kerrey, the labor support of Harkin, the sheer decency of Tsongas. A pinch of Bradley, a bit of Nunn and Gore and

Gephardt. And a dollop of regret, too, at all the good candidates who stayed out of the race and must be kicking themselves today.

Enough Identikit scenarios. Bill Clinton is going to be the Democratic candidate for president.

It's been a hard primary season, filled with questions. Mr. Clinton wasn't very good at some of the answers. He seemed to be doing a complicated minuet with his real self, the dance of the apologist for the person he once was. Over and over you hear about folks who are uncomfortable with him, who think he's too slick or too polished or just not quite quite. And then they meet him. And their opinion changes. Bill Clinton is obviously a guy who does better up close and personal. Still pictures and print quotes do him no service. They lack twang.

For months he'd been telling newspaper reporters that the American people have more important concerns than whom he's bedded, and it read like excuses, excuses, excuses. But when he threw it back at Phil Donahue, told him that they were going to be sitting in silence for a long time if this line of questioning continued, he won the audience in no time flat.

Donahue is just what Mr. Clinton needs, even if the political snobs think it's déclassé. That, and any other venue that lets him behave in a way local politicians do on a swing down Main Street. Mr. Clinton needs to shake the voters' hands and look into their eyes, at least metaphorically. He is good on many of the issues, although I'm still troubled by the fact that he took time out from campaigning to execute a brain-damaged murderer. And at least he knows what the issues are.

His empathy for the poor and the disfranchised seems genuine, the outgrowth of his own hardscrabble childhood and poor-boy-makes-good idealism. Racial polarization and crushing unemployment are much on his mind. He needs to communicate that concern to the people and, in the process, bring them Bill his own self. Ronald Reagan needed TV to abet a fantasy. Mr. Clinton needs it to communicate a reality.

It's time for a reality fix. It's time to get pragmatic. I hate pragmatism in politics, which perhaps should exempt me from this kind of job. Every four years I hope for an overweening idealism, perhaps the character flaw of someone whose first seminal political act was kneeling on a linoleum floor, saying the rosary with the sixth grade the day John F. Kennedy died.

But what I hate more than pragmatism is the idea of the Democrats expending their political capital on bickering and what-ifs, the idea of four years of disaffection with a White House that, now more than ever, seems to hover on some astroplane above the workaday world. It's funny; George Bush will have exactly the opposite problem that Bill Clinton does. Still pictures shelter him; behind a camera, his tangled syntax often makes him seem goofy or unconnected. He finds himself in an election in which it does not serve to seem too presidential, too privileged, too estranged from privation. Mr. Bush has to communicate that he is just plain folks.

And he can't even go on *Donahue*.

Bill Clinton is going to be the Democratic nominee for president. He's not perfect, but if you heed your history you discover that no candidate, not FDR, not JFK, ever has been. (You have to imagine poor Lincoln on the cover of *Time*—"I'm sorry, Agnes, but I could never vote for a man that ugly! And his wife is so unpleasant!") It no longer serves to compare him with Jerry Brown, or Paul Tsongas, or some fantasy man we yearned to embrace in the face of our natural disasters. This has been a season of hard questions, but at its end comes an easy one. Do you prefer George Bush?

GENDER
CONTENDER

July 8, 1992

To: Governor Clinton
Re: Half the Voters
Dear Governor, How's your sore throat? What's happening in the Pennsylvania primary? Is it my imagination or has Hillary been muzzled since the cookies vs. career controversy? Will Bob Kerrey be your running mate? There aren't any more bombshells, are there?

How come you haven't noticed us?

There are millions of agitated female voters out here and you have a golden opportunity to persuade us to support you. We're the people who upset Senator Alan J. Dixon in Illinois and could make Carol Moseley Braun the first woman of color to serve in the Senate. We're the people who have taken Lynn Yeakel from 0 to 60 in a couple of months in Pennsylvania, relishing the spectacle of a smart woman taking on Arlen Specter in a Senate race.

They say this is our year. The issues once called women's issues have become cutting-edge. Since this last momentous fall, when the Judiciary Committee sent Anita Hill back to Oklahoma like a doctoral candidate who had failed her orals, our anger has become a recognized national phenomenon. One of our fund-raising organizations, Emily's List, has doubled the number of its contributors since then.

Hasn't anyone told you?

We have no reason to support George Bush. Even some Republican women will say so. During the New Hampshire primary the reporters who cover the president got some yuks out of one commercial. In it, Mr. Bush was sitting at his desk when a woman assistant came in and handed him some papers. The joke was that it was the first woman assistant seen in the Oval Office since the administration began.

But it's not simply that Barbara Bush is the best-known woman in this administration. After all, your wife is the most prominent woman in your inner circle, too, although she has the experience to be part of a policy partnership as well as a domestic one. Your closest campaign advisers are the standard-issue white guys.

And this is not just about abortion. By the way, Governor, what was going through your mind last Wednesday? There was only one story in this country that day, and it was the future of legal abortion, writ large in Supreme Court arguments and in arrests in Buffalo. And you gave a speech about the environment. Great issue, bad timing, even if it was Earth Day.

Back in 1988 George Bush evoked significantly less enthusiasm from women than he did from men. And that was before he vetoed family leave, gagged the doctors at family-planning clinics, said Clarence Thomas was the best man for the job, and spent a year pretending that the economy was A-O.K. Opinion polls showed that we women were much less enamored of his antiseptic war in the Persian Gulf than our male counterparts.

You could fashion a victory out of this gender gap. If you are going to stand for a new generation, you can begin by standing for a generation that has come of age during the fight for equality at work and at home, a generation that has been irrevocably shaped by the changing roles, concerns, and problems of women. You could show that you get it, as the post-Hill shorthand goes. But first you have to convincingly recognize our existence.

You cannot assume that the gender gap automatically benefits you. You have a gender gap of your own, a personal one. Some women look at you and see every charming and evasive rover they ever had the bad fortune to tangle with.

You could defuse that if you spoke out in a constant and unremitting way about your commitment to family-planing clinics and prenatal care programs, family-leave policies and early-childhood-education initiatives, legal abortion and a polyglot inner circle. You've been out there romancing black voters, Jewish communities, labor unions. But you haven't romanced women enough. (Look, you're going to have this problem with double entendres. Just grin and bear it and everyone will think you're a sport.) We're raising hell in state races; we could raise hell in this one, too. But we're too ticked off to be taken for granted for long, and lots of us are still looking at you as the lesser of two evils, which doesn't inspire anybody to hire a sitter and trudge to the polls come November. The gool ol' boys keep saying you need to bring Joe Six-Pack back to the Democratic party in November. But for every Joe, there's another voter out there searching for a candidate. Name's Jane. We're waiting.

ALL OF THESE
YOU ARE

June 28, 1992

Let us begin today with the fact that being called a honky is not in the same league as being called a nigger.

And therein lies one explanation of why Bill Clinton generated considerable heat, but no light, when he publicly decried the anti-white comments of a woman by the name of Sister Souljah who thinks with her mouth.

This is not a meditation on the sister, who has already gotten more attention than her talents as a rap artist or a social commentator merit.

Nor is this a disquisition on the board game known as national politics and whether Governor Clinton wants to dis the Reverend Jesse Jackson, or to distance himself from him (although either, it seems to me, could have been covered adequately by a simple No when asked to speak).

This is about race, the thing today that dare not speak its name.

We not only lack the words. We lack the knowledge.

The Chicago bureau chief of *The New York Times,* Isabel Wilkerson, last week made this vivid by drawing word pictures of two neighboring communities. The dreams and aspirations of the people are much the same. But Roseland is black, Mount Greenwood white, as though Jim Crow had never died. One white woman said her family had to eat hamburger while the blacks bought steaks with their food stamps. She'd never actually seen anyone do this, you understand, but she knew that it was so.

The story observed: "The paradox, interviews show, is that black people were fearful because much of their contact with white people was negative; whites were fearful because they had little or no contact."

Into the fray in a nation so divided steps Mr. Clinton, sounding the white-guy clarion call, that hatred is as bad when it goes black to white as when it goes white to black. All things being equal, this is true.

Only all things aren't equal. Hatred by the powerful, the majority, has a different weight—and often very different effects—than hatred by the powerless, the minority. Reverse racism is like reverse discrimination: how much power does it really have in our overwhelmingly white world?

Mr. Clinton brought the Uzi of power and position to bear on someone with a dart gun full of poison. Those little suckers sure sting. But it's clear who's better armed. It's especially clear when the man should be carrying a lamp instead, looking to illuminate.

All of us rushed right in to say that Bill Clinton was right, right, right, no doubt about it. And there was no doubt that Sister Souljah's words have been unconscionable. But as any debater can tell you, right may give you a lovely puffed-up feeling, but sometimes it does not advance the argument.

Senator Bill Bradley took on this most difficult of issues in a speech in March. And he didn't do it with bromides, and he didn't do it because he was running for something, much as people wish he were. He talked about white fear of black criminality, he talked about the disintegration of the black family, he talked about misunderstanding and ill will on *all* sides, Republican and Democrat, white and black alike.

He told us we were all dependent on one another, and that if we do not stand united we will surely fall. Senator Bradley even said some of the things that Mr. Clinton was trying to say, talking about the "threats and bombast" of some black leaders. But he didn't single them out for blame. He asked us *all* to examine our consciences. He cast light.

This other has been pure heat. Sister Souljah got her fifteen minutes of fame. Jesse Jackson got to play his habitual game of Super Mario Brothers with the Democratic powers-that-be. And Mr. Clinton got to shout across from the white side of the racial divide that black folks can be racist, too. There are those who say he was pandering. If he prospers with the support of voters who believe that the key to racial problems in this country is blacks killing whites, or talking about killing whites, he will be little better than the current occupant of the job.

Our problem is not the venomous words of a rap singer—it is silences so huge we are drowning in them. Senator Bradley quoted Stephen Vincent Benét on the conundrum of America:

> All of these you are
> And each is partly you
> And none of them is false
> And none is wholly true.

Alas, it doesn't make for sound bites.

THE TWO FACES OF EVE

July 15, 1992

It is no longer the fashion to lie about the everyday lives of women. Gone are the days when we pretended that caring for children and cooking meals were an always rewarding enterprise. Gone are the days when we insisted that a real woman found it more satisfying to provide comfort for those who did great things in the world than to do great things in the world herself.

Now we only insist on lying about the lives of women whose husbands are running for president.

It's particularly noticeable this year, at this convention, as the Democrats parade their female congressional candidates, smart and outspoken and nobody's fools. It's particularly noticeable as Ann Richards runs the proceedings, a gavel, a grandmother, a governor. It's particularly noticeable as Barbara Jordan talks about the role of women in the party, and the party faithful, half of them female, roar back the joy of inclusion.

It's particularly noticeable that Hillary Clinton, who has already changed her name, her hair, her clothes, and her comments, is reduced to hawking her chocolate-chip-cookie entry in the First Lady bake-off.

What next? Eleanor Roosevelt fudge?

The irony is that if Ms. Clinton were up on that podium as a candidate, she would be golden, with her Yale Law degree, her board positions, her smarts, and her looks. But Hillary Rodham Clinton is running for First Lady, an anachronistic title for an amorphous position. The job description is a stereotype that no real woman has ever fit except perhaps June Cleaver on her good days.

The remarkable thing about how long the fantasy of the adoring and apolitical First Lady has endured is how few occupants of the job have conformed to it. In the last twenty-five years, only Pat Nixon has truly seemed separate from the work her husband made his life.

Margaret Truman Daniel, whose mother, Bess, was the prototype of First Lady as average American housewife, says she does not recall her parents talking politics much. But her husband, Clifton Daniel, demurs. "I heard her do it often," he said. "She was actively interested in politics and she did not hesitate to give her opinions."

Barbara Bush, she of the ubiquitous adjective "grandmotherly," has stoked the fiction afresh. In a fine profile in *Vanity Fair*, we learn how: she tends it relentlessly. "I could get in so much trouble if I said something she didn't agree with," her own stepmother worries. "Because you know how she is: she knows how she wants to appear to the world." And she knows how the world wants her to appear, canny Bar—not as the Machiavellian woman who can whip Bush subordinates into shape with a word, but as the happy shadow.

Mrs. Bush came of age when the best hope for advancement many women had was to hitch their wagon to their husband's star, although, like both Nancy Reagan and Rosalynn Carter, her lack of interest in influence is pure pulp fiction. Ms. Clinton is part of a different age, an age when we girls were taught we could be anything we chose—and were foolish enough to believe it. She is a lightning rod for the mixed emotions we have about work and motherhood, dreams and accommodation, smart women and men's worlds.

She was the kind of girl they said might wind up in the Oval Office. Now if she's lucky she'll get the East Wing, a not uncommon kind of pact in two-career marriages. Well, we say, she made her choices. She blonded and blended and sometimes she was outspoken and looked ambitious and that will never, ever do.

Here in New York and for the rest of this campaign we have the two faces of Eve. We have the women candidates, who are permitted—and I chose that word deliberately—to be ambitious, outspoken, strong, and sure.

And then we have Hillary Clinton, who must hawk those cookies and show off her daughter to prove her bona fide. Bill Clinton married someone smart and opinionated, who could challenge him and apparently frequently does. That's not an easy thing for a man, but apparently it's even tougher for this nation. Talk to people who don't like her and they often say they have never heard her speak or seen her interviewed. It is the idea of her they dislike.

Abigail Adams, a pistol if there ever was one, wrote in the famous "Remember the ladies" letter to her husband, John, the second president, "While you are proclaiming peace and good will to men, emancipating all nations, you insist upon retaining an absolute power over wives." It was a young country then. In some ways it still hasn't grown up.

THE FOURTH WALL

July 19, 1992

Late at night, bleached by the streetlights, the satellite dishes pale moons at its perimeter, Madison Square Garden looked like the starship *Enterprise*. The doors were barred to all but those with special passes by a phalanx of police officers, who stood between the arena and the uninvited—the protesters, the leafleteers, and the man who paced the corner repeating, "The answer is Jesus. Jesus is the answer."

The third night of the Democratic convention a man walked by with his hands in his pockets and muttered bitterly, "Blah blah blah blah." And though it is possible that he was not all there, this being New York City, the Democrats should keep in mind, during this anniversary celebration of the Michael Dukakis Memorial Euphoria, that he may have been an ordinary working Joe, giving vent to the still-considerable chasm between working Joes and politicos this country over.

Bill Clinton gave a speech Thursday night in which he introduced himself anew to the American people, making the per-

sonal political. The most important thing about that speech was
that he could not simply give it to the people in the Garden, the
people with the open-sesame passes slung around their necks.
Accepting the nomination of your party for the presidency is the
most egregious sort of exercise in preaching to the converted if
you talk to the folks in the hall.

Mr. Clinton needed to break the fourth wall, the barrier
between the actor and the audience, the scrim between the glib
circumlocutions of the stump speech and the yearning in ordinary Americans for recognition of the commonplace crises of
their lives. That is what he is going to have to do in the next four
months if he has a prayer of winning in November.

He is going to have to tell single parents about his plucky wid-
owed mom, tell working people about his grandfather's grocery
store. Contrast the universality of his biography with the narrow-
ness of George Bush's. Transcend the distance between the governed and the governors, a distance grown so great that it
seemed only a man who had never run for office could bridge it.

The lesson of Ross Perot's stillborn campaign is simple: Mr.
Perot was never a candidate, he was a wake-up call with ears.
Mario Cuomo, when he was trying to convince reporters of why
he need not run for president, used to say that it was not the messenger that was important, it was the message. In the case of the
Perot phenomenon that shoe fits. He was limited, this talk-show
wonder who got out when the going got tough. And he changed
the whole tenor of the race this year. When George Bush, who
seems to have been on a fishing trip for every major crisis of the
last four years, interrupts his angling to say that he got the message, something is out there. In his speech Mr. Clinton quoted
the civil rights activist Fanny Lou Hamer, who said when she was
running for Congress in 1964, "I'm sick and tired of being sick
and tired." Mr. Perot galvanized the sick-and-tired vote.

This last week there's been so much talk of positioning, a word
that is offensive to voters, suggesting that winning their alle-
giance requires no more than a Happy Meal with a McPrinciple

and a large middle ground. Mr. Clinton positioned himself as a moderate and friend of the middle class. He said it was time for a change in the party, to admit that the welfare system doesn't work and that creating jobs is more important than creating entitlements.

The Perot groundswell had nothing to do with positioning—there were few positions, even to the bitter end—and everything to do with a vast number of voters who believe that government and its citizens live in parallel universes. Paying seemly attention to the meaning of the Perot candidacy, Mr. Cuomo said in his nominating speech, "Before he told anyone what he intended to do or how he would do it, he used one word and the applause broke out all over America. The word was 'change'!"

That big broad vague message has preempted this election. The old Democratic stances have been muted and the theme of a new generation hammered home with everything from Elvis jokes to Fleetwood Mac anthems. The tone has been set: change. From here on in, Mr. Clinton must stand the dictum on its ear—the messenger has become critical, the messenger and his ability to look through the scrim of positioning and spin and electoral votes and simply say, "I see you. I know you. I am you."

ONE VIEW
FITS ALL

September 6, 1992

My oldest kid invited the jock home the other day. The jock's name is, of course, Kyle. He is a nice kid with an awesome arm, the kind who can choose a tree halfway down the road, pick up a stone, and—bing!—nail it while my son stands openmouthed.

This is one of the great rituals of growing up, trying to puzzle out who you are by discovering who you are not. Our children bring home familiar strangers, archetypes who will, by contrast, teach them what they're made of. There is something bittersweet about watching this, something that makes you want to give them simple answers instead of time and space. But figuring out who you are is the whole point of the human experience. So we let them be.

I couldn't help thinking of this when Pat Buchanan gave his hateful speech at the Republican convention. You figure when you go on vacation certain events will pass you by. But the Buchanan speech has stayed with me because it was so insulting to the American people and so contrary to everything we value.

The election, he said, "is about more than who gets what. It is about who we are." Here's the catch—who you are is who Pat Buchanan says you should be. Distrust differences. Revile people who are gay. Dismiss the aspirations of women. Reduce the answers to the problems of our cities to "force, rooted in justice, and backed by moral courage." Let your fears and hatreds be your guide. Invoke God to justify them.

"There is a religious war going on in this country for the soul of America," Mr. Buchanan said. And if you agree with him you are blessed. And if you do not you are damned.

Thus did we learn of a simpler life, life without thought.

Some Republicans were distressed by the us/them tone of Mr. Buchanan's speech. But his hyperpitch does not stand alone. Pat Robertson, who also spoke at the convention, says that the equal rights amendment "encourages women to leave their husbands, kill their children, practice witchcraft, destroy capitalism and become lesbians." (What? No cannibalism?) Marilyn Quayle, questioned about the wisdom of asking Mr. Buchanan to speak, said tight-lipped that he was the one who had done the asking. But Mrs. Quayle did some polarizing, too, saying liberals were "disappointed because women do not wish to be liberated from their essential natures as women." I don't know what Mrs. Quayle defines as my essential nature; luckily, I worked that one out for myself a long time ago. I know it will probably take my daughter some time and some pain to figure out what being female means to her. Guide her with my beliefs and experiences, sure, but I will not garrote her with them. Maybe it would be a lot less difficult if she followed some all-purpose formula. But then she'd be a lot less human.

In the weeks since the convention the Republicans have figured out what the rest of us were thinking as we sat in front of our televisions. They flogged this package they called family values. And you could almost hear millions of folks saying, "Guys, we'll take care of our values if you take care of the economy." And that is the point: we do take care of our own values, and it is

an insult to have some pol stand up and tell us he has a handy-
dandy all-purpose values package, one size fits all. The Republicans have now abandoned this campaign cul-de-sac. It would be
nice if this was because they realized it was wrong. The truth is it
just didn't play.

The Buchanan speech played least of all. Conscience is not
simple; prejudices are not ennobling. The problems of L.A.
require much more than automatic weapons. Good people disagree about abortion. Knowledge comes from discussion, not
conclusion and exclusion.

It is painful to watch our kids struggle to find themselves in a
complicated world. But it would be more painful still to have that
growth stunted by the kind of exclusionary and conclusory cate-
chism offered by Mr. Buchanan. He calls himself a traditionalist.
I am a traditionalist too. The tradition I cherish is the ideal this
country was built upon, the concept of religious pluralism, of a
plethora of opinions, of tolerance and not the jihad. Religious
war, pooh. The war is between those who trust us to think and
those who believe we must merely be led. Demagoguery vs.
democracy.

RUMOR HAS IT

October 11, 1992

The rumor moves quickly, from newspaper reporter to magazine writer to television correspondent and back again, in the whisper-down-the-lane world of journalism. Someone has said that Bill Clinton considered applying for citizenship in another country while trying to avoid the Vietnam draft.

But it had a smell about it, a tinny taste: no one had actually seen a letter that was said to exist, but a friend of a friend knew someone who had. First one newspaper was said to be preparing a page-one story, then another. Some versions said the approach was to the Swedes; others said it was to British officials.

I said Segretti.

Segretti is the word I mutter when my conscious mind refuses to accept the gutter level of politics in America. Donald Segretti was a dirty trickster of the Watergate era who, among other things, infiltrated the campaign of Edmund Muskie to make sure the capable Maine Democrat would crash and burn during the primary season.

There was the literature circulated during the Florida primary suggesting Senator Muskie supported Castro and forced busing. There were the stink bombs at appearances and the appearances mysteriously canceled. The coup de grace was the letter, on bogus Muskie campaign stationery, suggesting that Hubert Humphrey and Henry Jackson had engaged in sexual misconduct.

Sure enough, in 1972 George McGovern was the Democratic nominee, and Richard M. Nixon, on whose behalf Mr. Segretti labored, won by a landslide.

This would all be history if the president had not revealed in the last few days that he is living in the past, and the worst sort of past at that.

It is astounding that Mr. Bush says that demonstrating against the Vietnam War, an honorable way for millions of us to register righteous dissent, was a dishonorable undertaking. It is astounding that he would suggest, with not a shred of evidence, that a trip Mr. Clinton made as a student to Russia was suspect.

When Representative Robert Dornan, a stalking horse for the Bush campaign, said Mr. Clinton had gone to Moscow as a guest of the K.G.B., he didn't even bother to concoct sources, as Mr. Segretti might have done in the old days. Mr. Dornan said he had no proof; he just thought it was so.

Like most rumors, it is impossible to trace the one about Mr. Clinton's citizenship to its source. The State Department certainly helped the rumor along by referring questions about alleged tampering with Mr. Clinton's passport file to the F.B.I., the ultimate red flag. No one has explained how the State Department came to be looking at Mr. Clinton's file in the first place, since it is protected by privacy laws and cannot be reviewed without his consent.

And no one has explained why a young man so ambitious that he wrote at twenty-three that he could not resist the draft and "maintain my political viability" would consider renouncing American citizenship. No one has to explain—it's just a rumor, right? Nevertheless, Mr. Clinton has been placed in the position of having to deny it on several talk shows. He has also had to deny that his Russian trip included anything untoward. Thus does the rumor mill grind.

Mr. Bush miscalculates, and miscalculates again. With his attacks on Mr. Clinton's dissent during the Vietnam era, he insults a huge group of Americans who believed the policy in Southeast Asia was ill conceived. And he revives the Silent Majority divide-and-conquer strategy of Mr. Nixon, a strategy that was ultimately devalued by a growing body of opinion hostile to the war and the historical record on the corruption within the Nixon administration.

The innuendo campaign about the Clinton trip and the Clinton antiwar activity makes it clear that the Bush campaign is both desperate and desperately out of touch. When the debates begin tonight, I hope the president remembers that most of us are living in 1992.

Mr. Bush is stuck in a time warp, part *Best Years of Our Lives,* part Joe McCarthy. As he has done so often during this campaign, he has now backed off from his criticism of the Moscow trip, not because it was dishonest but because it didn't play. And the F.B.I. announced Friday that it had ended its investigation into Mr. Clinton's passport file without finding evidence of tampering. Thus does the rumor mill run out. It all stinks to high heaven; it all smells of desperation, but not of votes. Mr. Bush needs to get current and win friends. As Mr. Nixon could tell him, fighting dirty can be a chancy way to make them.

A PLACE CALLED HOPE

November 4, 1992

For the last fifteen years Barbara Walters has been haunted by
the comment she made to Jimmy Carter in a pre-inaugural interview. "Be wise with us," she said. "Be good to us." The truth is that
we all know what she meant, because most of us, on one Tuesday
in November or another, have felt at least a whiff of the same
thing. It's called hope.

I flipped the little blackjack next to Bill Clinton's name with
hope, the first time I recall feeling that emotion since I cast my
first vote for George McGovern in 1972. If ever a man has been
tested for the presidency, it is this one, not in Vietnam or even in
the trenches of long life, but in the court of public opinion.

My polling place was choked with voters; even children wanted
to stay up and hear the news. Everyone is eager to say that this is
because the American people seized the day. And they did, fash-
ioning a real contest from common sense, Larry King, the
debates, the *MacNeil/Lehrer Newshour,* the pages of their newspa-

pers, the *Today* show, endless dinner-table discussions, and concern for their children and their checkbooks.

In time there will be many postmortems of this election, but one thing they should all have in common is the admission that Bill Clinton ran the best Democratic campaign in recent memory, and George Bush the worst Republican one. The man who was inexorable vs. the man who didn't turn up, then turned nasty. History will record that the president turned in two lackluster debate performances and that when he got his campaign back on course with questions about higher taxes and misplaced trust, he derailed it himself by the sophomoric gaffe of calling his opponents "bozos" and comparing their expertise to that of his spaniel. They say it's not over till the fat lady sings; I say when the dogs rear their heads, it's time to bow-wow out.

But ultimately the president's greatest burden was his own first term. On the morning after Franklin Delano Roosevelt was elected president in 1932, the editorial page of this paper thundered: "The Republicans got what they richly deserved. During the past 12 years they have displayed that insensate pride which goeth before destruction. . . . Four years ago Republicans promised, under their benign guidance, an ever-ascending scale of prosperity, just before the worst and longest financial and industrial and agricultural disaster fell upon the land." And the editorial added, "There can be no mistaking the determination of the American electorate to order a change in their government and in its policies." I am a working mother, a feminist, and a reporter whose enduring interest has been in the small moments of the lives of unsung people, the kind of people who ride in limos only when someone in the family dies. I thought George Bush was not interested in, not even aware of, most of those disparate parts of my life, whether vetoing family leave, nominating Clarence Thomas, or talking endlessly about a capital gains tax.

One night I saw Bill Clinton on the news say, "The hits that I took in this election are nothing compared to the hits the people

of this state and this country have been taking for a long time."
And I began to believe that he saw us. I began to believe that
growing up struggling to make ends meet, learning to live with
an alcoholic parent, losing the governor's office because of the
hubris of the young and cocky, and taking the hits about
infidelity, patriotism, and moral spine that he had taken during
this campaign might have taught him something about hard
times.

Every once in a while I want a little hope, the way some people
want a martini or a new pair of shoes. That's what Barbara Walters was trying to get at when she talked to Jimmy Carter. People
said she didn't act like a journalist, and maybe there's some truth
in that. But maybe there are simply some occasions when we
reporters, despite our best intentions, can't help acting like
human beings.

Yesterday was one of them. I could be cynical about the possibility of real change and the manifest dangers of expectations. I
could talk about the enormous challenges to come. But not right
now. This is Mr. Clinton's moment; he deserves it and I am glad
he prevailed. You walk into the voting booth and each time you
pull the little lever there is implicit in the gesture a tiny leap of
faith. And this time some hope as well. For at least a moment, I'll
make it last.

WOMEN'S
RITES

I f anyone had told me even ten years ago that I would, in my first years as an Op-Ed columnist, write more columns about abortion that any other single subject, I would have been both incredulous and disconcerted. The reasons are obvious. I am Catholic. I have three beloved children whose gestation, delivery, and rearing have been my greatest joy. And I have been, for most of my life, deeply ambivalent about abortion, about what it is, what it means, and how we think about it.

None of those things changed during the time that I wrote an opinion column. But what they came to mean to me within the context of the unquenchable fire of the abortion debate that raged in America during the last decade of the twentieth century changed a good deal.

The truth is that no matter what I had eventually come to believe, think, and feel about the subject, I would have been remiss in my mandate as an opinion columnist, and particularly as a woman in the job, if I had not written with some regularity about the subject. Only think: during 1990, 1991, and 1992 Supreme Court justices were apparently chosen on the basis of their perceived positions on the issue, several American cities were thrown into tumult because of demonstrations about it, it became a defining issue in a presidential campaign, and the Supreme Court handed down one of its most important and eloquent opinions on the subject. No one can claim it is an exaggeration to say that abortion became the most talked about and controversial issue in this country during the 1990s. And that shows no signs of abating.

"When do you think it will be settled?" people sometimes ask. And I think the answer is clear: it will never be settled. That alone makes it an issue different from most others, and more compelling, too.

But for me it is also the issue that most embodies the name that was eventually cooked up for my column when we began it in 1990. It took us a long, long time to find a name. We would think something sounded right, send it to the legal department to be vetted, and find out that some other publication was already using it. (The best blowout was the name "Persuasion," which I floated primarily because I am a great Jane Austen fan. It turned out that "Persuasion" was already the name of a column— an advice column in a sadomasochistic skin mag.)

The editorial-page editor, Jack Rosenthal, finally came up with the name "Public & Private" modeled, in part, after Walter Lippmann's "Today and Tomorrow." At first I found it serviceable but not particularly illuminating; eventually I found it perfect. For I became most interested in writing about the intersection of the private and the public, most convinced that that was where the action was. The economy as reflected in the job search by a fifty year-old middle-management type, the issues of welfare dependency embodied in one reluctant welfare mother—the policy without the personal seemed to me empty, the personal without the political not telling enough. The two together spoke the truth.

And nowhere is this more true than on the question of who will and should decide whether an individual pregnancy must be taken to its endpoint of birth and motherhood. It was because of my private feelings that my public profile became so determinedly that of an advocate for legal abortion.

(A word on words here: the words we use to talk about abortion are among the most unsatisfactory in any public dialogue. Both pro-life and pro-choice are oversimplifications, and nothing about this issue is simple. So at a certain point I tried to give up both and simply refer to the two groups as those opposed to legal abortion, and those in favor of it. This adds words and, when 750 is your limit, added words are unhappy events. But the alternative was distortion by oversimplification, which is, to my mind, no alternative at all.)

My Catholicism has in fact guided me to that position, because it first led me to the idea that the act of an individual examining her conscience to search for wrongdoing was honorable and proper. My three children, while the greatest joy of my life, were all wanted but exhausting, so that, having them and rearing them, I felt conscious of the potential damage to both mother and child of an unwanted pregnancy in a way I doubted many of the male leaders of the movement against abortion, so blithe in their assumption that one could make do, would ever be.

But above all it is my continuing questioning and various ambivalences about the issue that have, paradoxically, brought me down most heavily on one side of the wall that seems to exist between those who favor legal abortion and those who do not. Some will be surprised by that; others will find it false. The profile of most feminists on the issue—and I am feminist, have been nearly all my sentient life—is that we believe flatly that women cannot be free unless they can control when they will carry a pregnancy to term. In some broad sense this is correct; in many ways it is an oversimplification, ignoring the complexity of one of our most complex questions.

I have never sat down to write about abortion without feeling, at least for a moment, the complexities sweep over me like a fit of faintness: the complete life of the woman and the burgeoning life of the child, the primitive development of the embryo and the potential traits of the baby, the joy a pregnancy often brings and the despair it sometimes carries with it.

There is no other issue that so often and so insistently forces me to wrestle with who I am, with what I believe; even when I still went into the dark cabinet of the confessional every single Saturday, I never examined my conscience as I do when I choose, often with a sigh and a sense of the futility of meaningful discourse, to write about abortion. The process of argument itself has taught me something about this most private of public issues, and that is that the most suitable battlefield upon which to play out its vast conundrums is the one inside my soul.

THE ABORTION ACCOUNT

April 8, 1990

When I was growing up, my life was governed by nuns and priests. Don't scratch in public, Sister said. Don't roll your skirt up, Sister said. Don't whisper in class. Don't gossip. Don't cheat.

The priests were always more remote. What I remember best is the outline of their profiles against the confessional screen and the low murmur as they repeated the words of absolution while I said my act of contrition. In a church so often devoted to conformity and crowds, this seemed the great individual act, the confession of the soul, examining her conscience.

The solitary claustrophobia of the confessional came back to me last week when American Catholic bishops announced their new campaign against abortion. They are prepared to spend as much as $5 million to convince the people of this country that their most bitterly contested right is a mortal sin. A powerful public relations firm and the pollsters who brought us Ronald Reagan have been hired to succeed where sermons failed. Examinations of conscience give way to examining the efforts of slick professional persuaders. For years we have bemoaned the hat trick with mirrors these people have made out of the ballot box. Now we admit them to the pulpit.

My heart sinks.

Five million dollars. My God, the good we could do with $5 million. The women carrying wanted babies who cannot afford the meat and milk to nourish them in utero. The babies just born who stare at the ceiling in hospital nurseries, waiting for some-one to take them home, even to touch them for more than a few minutes. The babies born fifty years ago who now live in subway tunnels and cardboard boxes and the doorways outside the resi-dence of John Cardinal O'Connor, who announced this cam-paign. If this is such an honorable battle, why did no polling group, no public relations outfit, offer its services free so we could spend this money on babies already born?

I don't mean to suggest that the Church does not help the dis-franchised. The sad state of affairs today is that the compassion and intelligence of many priests and nuns and laymen are lost in the din surrounding the pronouncements of a very few. All over this city Catholics educate, feed, and house the poor. But they work unsung while we listen to Cardinal O'Connor speak of the dangers of heavy-metal music. It seems such a minor issue in a city where human suffering screams louder than any boom box.

I do understand why the bishops have decided to do this. Around this issue all the frustration of conservative Catholic clergy has coalesced, the frustration they must experience every Sunday when they walk onto the altar and know they've lost them in the pews. For two decades they have looked out and seen Catholics who have gone their own way on premarital sex, birth control, divorce, and abortion, too. If they threw them all out, the churches would be denuded.

Some Catholics would argue that I did not learn the most important lesson from my Catholic education: the Church makes the rules. Sister taught us that the priests were always right. But the Catholics who were children then are adults now. And many of them seem to have learned best what I did, the examination of conscience, the searching of the soul to discover whether they had done wrong.

I do not believe the bishops understand the abortion issue, and not only for the obvious reason that they will never be pregnant or have a wife or daughter who is. It reminds me of all those years when our mothers came to them in the confessional and quietly pleaded: Five children in seven years, Father. Isn't it enough? Isn't there something that can be done? No one does that anymore. We already know the answers. Abstinence, abstinence, abstinence. This is how they lost us in the pews. They refused to look at our lives.

The same is true today. They do not listen. The most notable exception is the archbishop of Milwaukee, Rembert G. Weakland, who, while his colleagues were loudly warning Mario Cuomo of hell, was quietly asking Catholic women on both sides of the divisive issue to come together and talk. He wanted them to listen to one another, and he wanted to listen to them all.

His actions suggest the Church still honors its people.

A multimillion-dollar payout to public relations and polling firms suggests something quite different. It tells those women convinced they are the best guardians of their own bodies that the Church believes they are shallow enough to be swayed by practiced paid persuasion, as though they were buying soap powder. It suggests that the bishops no longer see us as souls, but as votes. And in a country where people dine from Dumpsters, it is a monumental waste of money.

MOM, DAD, AND ABORTION

July 1, 1990

Once I got a fortune cookie that said: To remember is to understand. I have never forgotten it. A good judge remembers what it was like to be a lawyer. A good editor remembers what it was like to be a reporter.

A good parent remembers what it was like to be a child.

I remember adolescence, the years of having the impulse control of a mousetrap, of being as private as a safe-deposit box.

And I've remembered it more keenly since the Supreme Court ruled that the states may require a pregnant minor to inform her parents before having an abortion.

This is one of the most difficult of many difficult issues within the abortion debate. As good parents, we remember being teenagers, thinking that parents and sex existed in parallel universes.

But as good parents, it also seems reasonable to wonder why a girl who cannot go on a school field trip without our knowledge can end a pregnancy without it.

The Supreme Court found succor in a Minnesota law that provides for something called "judicial bypass." If you are fifteen and want to have an abortion but cannot tell your parents—the law provides that both must be informed, not simply one—you can tell it to the judge. You come to the clinic, have an exam and counseling. Then you go to the courthouse, meet with a public defender and go to the judge's chambers, to be questioned about your condition, your family, your plans for the future.

If the judge agrees, you can have the abortion.

The Court did not find this an undue burden for a frightened fifteen-year-old.

Tina Welsh, who runs the only abortion clinic in Duluth, remembers the first girl she took to the courthouse when the law went into effect. The young woman did not want to notify her father; he was in jail for having sex with her sister. Ms. Welsh remembers taking girls up in the freight elevator because they had neighbors and relations working in the courthouse. You can just hear it:

"Hi, sweetheart, how are you? What brings you here?"

So much for the right to privacy.

But Ms. Welsh best remembers the young woman who asked, "How long will the jury be out?" She thought she was going on trial for the right to have an abortion.

Much of this debate centers, like the first sentence of *Anna Karenina,* on happy families, and unhappy ones. Abortion-rights activists say parental notification assumes a world of dutiful daughters and supportive parents, instead of one riven by alcoholism, incest, and abuse. Those opposed to abortion say it is unthinkable that a minor child should have such a procedure without her parents' knowledge.

But I remember something between the poles of cruelty and communication. I remember girls who wanted their parents to have certain illusions about them. Not girls who feared beatings, or were pregnant by their mother's boyfriend. Just girls who wanted to remain good girls in the minds that mattered to them most.

Ms. Welsh remembers one mother who refused to let her husband know their daughter was having an abortion. "Twenty-five years ago," the woman said, "we made a promise to one another. I would never have to clean a fish, and he would never have to know if his daughter was pregnant."

If parental-notification laws are really designed to inhibit abortion—and I suspect they are—Ms. Welsh's experience suggests they are not terribly successful. Not one teenager who came to the Duluth clinic changed her mind, even in the face of public defenders and judicial questioning. If the point is to facilitate family communication, that's been something of a failure, too. In the five years the Minnesota law was in effect, seven thousand minors had abortions. Half of those teenagers chose to face a stranger in his chambers rather than tell both parents.

But perhaps there is another purpose to all this. If adolescents want their parents to have illusions about them, parents need those illusions badly. These laws provide them. They mandate communication. If she has nothing to tell you, then it must mean nothing is wrong.

Ah, yes—I remember that.

These are difficult questions because they involve not-quite adults facing adult decisions. The best case is the daughter who decides, with supportive parents, whether to end a pregnancy or have a baby. The worst case is the girl who must notify the parent who impregnated her. Or the worst case is Becky Bell, a seventeen-year-old Indianapolis girl who died after an illegal abortion. She could not bear to tell her parents she was pregnant.

In the middle are girls who have been told by the Supreme Court that they must trade. They can keep a good-girl persona at home, but in exchange they must surrender some of their privacy and dignity. That is what adults want, and that is what we will have. We will take our illusions. The teenagers will take the freight elevator.

THE NUNS' STORY

September 16, 1990

Barbara Ferraro and Patricia Hussey are no longer nuns. They did not leave the convent as so many others did, finding fulfillment within the smaller circle of marriage and motherhood. These two spent years finding reasons to stay: to serve the poor, to fight for social justice. They resigned from the Sisters of Notre Dame in 1988, four years after a full-page advertisement appeared in *The New York Times* under this headline:

A DIVERSITY OF OPINIONS REGARDING ABORTION EXISTS AMONG COMMITTED CATHOLICS.

Ninety-seven people signed it.

Barbara Ferraro and Patricia Hussey were two of them.

They have written a book about what happened after that day, and what their lives were like before it. It is called *No Turning Back,* and it is sure to be seen as an attack on the Church. That oversimplifies its most important message, contained in an anecdote about Barbara's encounter at a poor parish in Massachusetts. A woman blurted out, "Sister, I had an abortion five years ago." Barbara Ferraro was stunned. Finally she said, "Tell me about it."

Tell me about it. Tell me about the thing I have never experienced and cannot begin to understand. Tell me, as one of the girls did at the juvenile home where Pat Hussey worked, about the biker's initiation rite, the gang rape that left you pregnant. Tell me, as that woman told Barbara, of the abortion when your marriage was falling apart and the children you already had were as many as you could support. Tell me about the lives I haven't led, the demons I've never faced.

Barbara Ferraro and Pat Hussey stayed in the convent because they saw it changing. When Barbara entered in 1962, she was given a habit that left only her face and hands uncovered. Her hair was shorn, her name was changed, and she was given a whip to discipline herself. By the time she resigned, she was wearing slacks and running a homeless shelter.

In between she learned that "Tell me about it" would never be the motto of the Church to which she had given her life. Those nuns who signed the ad were given a choice: Retract or face dismissal. Barbara and Pat were eventually confronted by a Vatican representative and an apostolic Pro-Nuncio in Washington. The former pinched Barbara's cheek and told her she reminded him of his grandmother. The latter said they would have a dialogue. "But I must insist," he said, "that after our time together you must put in writing that you support and adhere to the Roman Catholic teaching on abortion."

They couldn't do it. They had had too many women tell them about it.

The Church is not a democracy. The editorial-page editor of *The Philadelphia Inquirer,* David Boldt, referred to it several months ago as "un-American," and was vilified by Catholics, from parishioners to cardinals. What he meant was that it is not democratic. The people cannot vote on Church positions. The decisions are made by the men at the top.

They are uniquely unqualified to face the most pressing issues of their time. Birth control, the ordination of women, permission for priests to marry, abortion—all arise from sexuality and femininity. The primacy of the priesthood rests upon celibacy and masculinity. The Catholic bishops in this country decided last week to postpone indefinitely a final vote on a pastoral letter on women's concerns. It is born to fail, a précis on women written by men who haven't lived with one since they left their mother's house.

Last week, too, Judge David H. Souter was questioned by the Senate Judiciary Committee. "Souter archaeology," they had been calling it the last time I was in Washington, and they had come up with barely a pottery shard on abortion. During the hearings Judge Souter said two things that captured my attention. He said as a young man he once spent two hours in a college dorm room talking to a young woman who was desperate to end a pregnancy. And he said, "What you may properly ask is whether I am open to listen."

Tell me about it.

Barbara Ferraro and Pat Hussey judged the hierarchy of the Catholic Church on that basis. "The Vatican's version of Catholicism is a culture of oppression," they write, "a church that is only about itself." Those are harsh words. These are harsh times. And faced with harsh laws of Church and of state, women like these will continue to speak, no matter what the consequences.

Barbara Ferraro and Pat Hussey shouldn't have been nuns in the first place.

They should have been priests.

OFFENSIVE PLAY

January 24, 1991

On Sunday the Super Bowl will be played in Tampa, and so, inevitably, my thoughts turn to abortion.

If that seems like a preposterous connection, it is only because you have not seen *Champions for Life*, the video featuring scenes from the New York Giants' last Super Bowl victory and six members of that championship team talking about their blocking, their passing, and their opposition to legal abortion. It might be reminiscent of *Saturday Night Live* if it weren't so offensive.

"The skies were sunny, the temperature a comfortable seventy-six degrees," says the narrator as we-came-to-play music is heard in the background. Fans wave pompons. Players take to the field. "What follows are a few highlights from the game and some comments from the champions."

Mark Bavaro catches a pass, then appears in street clothes to say: "At the end of the game all the Giants players left the field champions. Now with the abortion death squads allowed to run rampant through our country, I wonder how many future champions will be killed before they see the light of day."

George Martin sacks John Elway in the end zone. His thoughts? "I'm glad I was able to help turn the tide in the Super Bowl with that safety. I hope and pray that the Supreme Court has begun to turn the tide against the legalized destruction of babies allowed by the *Roe* v. *Wade* decision. That infamous decision said that unborn babies have no rights just as the shameful Dred Scott decision said that black people have no rights."

And Phil Simms, musing on his record-breaking day: "When I woke up the next morning and read those statistics in the paper, I was very pleased and proud. But there was another statistic in the paper that morning that didn't get the same coverage the Super Bowl got. I guess they thought it wasn't very important. It was just a little item that stated there are an average of forty-four hundred babies killed every day by abortion."

I've left out Phil McConkey, Chris Godfrey, and Jim Burt. They've left out women; the word is not used once during the ten-minute film. But you get the idea. Abortion and football— you just can't separate them. The video ends with the question "If the abortionists had their way, which two of these Giants might never have had the chance to be champions?"

It had never occurred to me that this was a central issue in the debate over reproductive freedom.

Wellington Mara, an owner of the team, was the guiding spirit behind *Champions for Life*. He is one of its producers and says he was largely responsible for financing it. The American Life League, an anti-abortion group based in Virginia, which distributes the video, has sent it to hundreds of organizations. Their records show that the Archdiocese of Los Angeles alone bought almost three hundred copies, some to be shown in schools to kids who may think the words "quarterback" and "god" are synonymous. The players who appear volunteered.

That's no surprise. We've become accustomed to movie actors and bass guitarists who believe that notoriety has given them a flair for geopolitics. But whether or not a pregnant woman should be allowed to end a pregnancy is a serious, complicated subject. Using football wrapped around self-righteous bromides to sell opposition to legal abortion is a little like using sex to sell cigarettes. It's permissible. And it's unseemly. Like the moment in the video when Jim Burt holds his young son on his shoulders and the kid says, in a way I assume is meant to sound unscripted, "It's great to be alive."

There are surely fans, men and women seen cheering wildly on that tape, who would be appalled to discover that they are part of such an effort. Deborah Kent, a hypnotherapist who was once such a megafan that she was profiled in the sports pages of this paper and who was sent a copy of the video after complaining to Mr. Mara about it, now says, "Whenever I see Mark Bavaro I hope he drops the ball."

Of the players who made *Champions for Life*, only Mr. Bavaro will play Sunday. Phil Simms is injured, Jim Burt plays for San Francisco, and the other three are retired. But Mr. Mara remains co-owner of the team, and he remains devoted to this cause. So while you may look out over the field and see a spectacular pass, a tragic fumble, a triumphant run into the end zone, he may envision a colorful and lively backdrop for another ten-minute sermonette linking athletic prowess and moral superiority. It's his right to do that. I just think it's out of bounds.

RUST, ROE, AND REALITY

July 17, 1991

I never thought I would have a good word to say about *Rust* v. *Sullivan*, the ridiculous Supreme Court decision upholding regulations barring doctors in federally financed clinics from discussing abortion with pregnant patients.

But the advantage is in the adjective. It seems to me that many Americans who paid no mind to abortion rights have been perplexed by the ridiculous nature of the ruling. (It has also generated terrific editorial cartoons, cartoonists being among our finest commentators. I can't decide which I prefer, the one of the doctor with a gavel in his mouth, or the one of the clinic sign: The Supreme Court has prohibited us from informing you that having an ABORTION IS A LEGAL ALTERNATIVE.)

The universe that once consisted only of those of us who might need an abortion or have friends and relations who might need one was enlarged to include those who have asked a physician for complete information. "I don't like the idea of abortions," one elderly woman said, "but a doctor should have to tell you the truth, even if there's politics involved."

This expansion of the universe, this recognition that politics has no place in a doctor's office, this appreciation of the ridiculous provisions of a federal gag rule, may come in handy in the future. What was once a what-if has now become a how-soon: the Supreme Court as constituted by Ronald Reagan and George Bush is a total loss in terms of reproductive freedom, and next term there is considerable likelihood that it will overturn *Roe* v. *Wade.* Whether Clarence Thomas is confirmed or not probably makes little difference. The president is not going to turn around and nominate Laurence Tribe instead.

If it is true, as polls tell us over and over again, that the American people believe abortion is a private matter, they will now have to prove it in the voting booth. They will have to press their elected representatives for federal law ensuring the right to an abortion. Failing that, they will have to push legislators to make abortion legal in their states, and elect legislators who will do so.

State courts have begun to move into the breach. Eight have found a right to privacy that includes reproductive choice within their state constitutions. In New York the Court of Appeals will consider that issue this fall when it hears arguments in a challenge by the New York Civil Liberties Union of Medicaid-funding bans. The case is *Hope* v. *Perales:* Hope for short, and for sure.

Alternatives to constitutional protection will be neither easy nor ideal. The courts are meant to be places of principle, but the legislatures are bastions of compromise. Legislative guarantees are likely to come with strings attached. Parental notification. Waiting periods. With state-by-state action, geography is destiny. A state constitutional right to privacy in New York is cold comfort to a girl in Louisiana who doesn't have bus fare. All the jockeying, the lobbying, the campaigning will be quietly enraging for those who believe that what may be growing within them is uniquely their own business, not the business of a lot of men in suits.

The what-if is upon us. You'd think the Republican leadership, which incorporated opposition to legal abortion in the party platform in 1980, would be jumping up and down. The reaction has been somewhat different. The uproar over *Rust* v. *Sullivan* has been so considerable, and the House rejection of clinic restrictions by a 353-to-74 vote so decisive, that the president said last week he might be amenable to some compromise. And just a few days ago the Young Republican National Federation considered removing an anti-abortion plank from its platform. Many delegates at the group's convention thought the position was a political liability.

Interesting that that should happen now, that some political opposition softens as the removal of the constitutional protection draws nearer. Many women have thought of *Roe* as an umbrella, sheltering our rights. But it has protected politicians, too, from the necessity of taking a stand anywhere but behind the podium. It will be interesting to see if George Bush will maintain his manufactured opposition to legal abortion if it means not merely appointing conservative jurists to the country's highest court, but vetoing federal legislation and thereby directly, conclusively denying the right of choice to millions of women. Who vote.

HIDDEN AGENDAS

August 10, 1992

At first glance there is something terribly confusing about what is going on in the life of Patrick F. Kelly, a federal judge in Wichita, Kansas, who may be wondering why he didn't go to dental school. Judge Kelly has forbidden members of Operation Rescue, the anti-abortion search-and-destroy group, to block access to abortion clinics in town.

In return, his jurisprudence has been attacked by his own government and his life has been threatened. One man reportedly left a message on the judge's home answering machine, describing how his body would be dismembered after he was killed.

Now, let me get this straight: it's wrong to destroy an embryo, but it's O.K. to kill a full-grown federal judge.

Judge Kelly hasn't had much to do with the abortion issue in his eleven years on the federal bench, but he's getting a fast and dirty education since Operation Rescue decided to make Wichita a high-profile battleground. And the judge is discovering an essential truth of the movement: things are not always the way they seem. Getting a death threat from a person who pretends a keen interest in the right to life is the least of the contradictions.

The intervention in this matter by the Justice Department is described by officials as simply a dispute over the Ku Klux Klan Act of 1871, which allows federal courts to protect a class of people from conspiracies to violate their civil rights. Judge Kelly relied on that law when he sent in federal marshals to safeguard entrances at the clinics. He also promised to jail anyone who defied his order—even the governor.

Operation Rescue lawyers argued that the 1871 act doesn't apply, and the Justice Department supported them in an amicus brief. Amicus means friend, and that's exactly what Justice is being to the anti-abortion folks, talking jurisdictional disputes and playing politics. President Bush continues to court the right-to-life vote, and Attorney General Dick Thornburgh, who turned in his resignation yesterday, is running for the U.S. Senate in Pennsylvania. Most of what we need to know about Justice Department intervention in this case is contained in election contests, not legal papers.

So many men, so little candor. Randall Terry, who runs Operation Rescue, has been most honest when he has talked about the proper subservient role of women in society. His colleagues wear tiny fetus-feet lapel pins. But what some of them seem to oppose is not abortion but the rise of individualism and the changing roles of women. When they talk about innocent life, they are talking about what they see as a more innocent time, when the same moral strictures applied to everyone, when gay people were in the closet, sex resulted in conception, and women stayed at home.

In her book *Abortion and the Politics of Motherhood*, the sociologist Kristin Liker describes the abortion battle as a referendum, a conflict between those who think raising children is one part of a woman's life, freely chosen, and those who think it is the center of a woman's life, her essential destiny. Supporters of legal abortion often say that their opponents are not interested in women, only the unborn. But some of those opponents are keenly interested in maintaining traditional roles, in pushing back the tide of change.

Like all the other abortion battles, at base the one in Wichita is about how we live now. It's hard to see how the man who threatens to cut Judge Kelly into little pieces is choosing life. Instead I would imagine that he is enraged that others are choosing a life of which he does not approve.

The administration has chosen to support that sort of rage, and thousands of protesters are throwing one American town into a tumult to vent it. The Justice Department sent them a message; while the entrances to the clinics cleared in the wake of Judge Kelly's order, the demonstrators were back yesterday, trying their best to inhibit women from exercising a clear constitutional right.

It seems contradictory that liberals are demanding law and order and conservatives are justifying disruptive protests. But that is no more contradictory than the rest of this sorry episode, in which the so-called Department of Justice sides with the lawbreakers, and those who march beneath the banners that say CHOOSE LIFE deny others their choice and disrupt the lives of thousands.

THE ABORTION ORPHANS

February 19, 1992

The photograph on the postcard is of a Gibson girl, hair piled atop her head, lace on her rounded shoulders, and a face in profile that is not so much pretty as soft and very young. Beneath the picture are these words:

CLARA BELL DUVALL WAS A 32-YEAR-OLD MOTHER OF FIVE WHEN SHE DIED OF AN ILLEGAL ABORTION IN 1929.

On the other side is written in a strong slanting hand, "My mother in her wedding picture at 18 years of age."

"The image of her in her casket is seared in my brain," said Linn Duvall Harwell, who had just turned six when her mother died.

The hospital listed the cause of death as "pneumonia."

She used a knitting needle.

She had a son and four daughters.

"She was a beautiful mother," says Mrs. Harwell. "That must be understood. She was loving and affectionate. We were poor and it was 1929, but we were cared for. The minute she died, it all changed."

"I can't help but think how my life would have been different," says Gwendolyn Elliot, who is a commander in the Pittsburgh Police Department. She was five when Vivian Campbell, her mother, died in 1950; she and her brother were raised by their grandparents. When she was eighteen and ready for college, she tried to cash in some bonds her mother had left her and was told she needed a death certificate. And there it was, under cause of death: the word "abortion," followed by a question mark.

The abortion orphans may be the shadow of things to come. Those of us who believe that abortion must remain legal are flailing about for a way to make vivid what will happen if it is banned once more. We have had the right so long that we have forgotten what the wrong is. Meant to evoke bloodstained tables and covert phone calls, the term "back alley" does not resonate for women who grew up with clean clinics and licensed doctors.

But there is indeed a kind of endless alley in the lives of Linn Harwell and Gwen Elliot, the dead end in your heart when you grow up without a mother. They tell us something about banning abortion that is both touching and chilling, these two little girls who grew up to become activists because of what happened to them. Which likely means many little girls, and boys, too, who do not know, who still believe pneumonia did it, or who are ashamed, who keep the secret.

This is the shadow of things to come. Someone's mother will die. That's not how we commonly think of this. We usually think of children having children, even though statistics show more than half of the abortions performed in the United States last year were performed on women over the age of twenty-five.

We think of cases like the horrific one unfolding in Ireland right now, in which a fourteen-year-old girl who says she was raped has been forbidden by the courts to travel to England to have an abortion. Her parents made a critical mistake: they were good citizens. They asked police about having fetal-tissue tests done as evidence. The attorney general stepped right in to enjoin the girl's planned abortion.

It is a great mistake to believe that if abortion is illegal, it will be nonexistent. Ireland has the most restrictive abortion laws in Europe, and still several thousand of its citizens travel elsewhere to end their pregnancies each year.

Some kind of douche, some kind of drug, some kind of tubing: women will do it themselves. They always have. They become pregnant for reasons we know nothing of, reasons not as easily quantifiable as being raped by a friend's father at age fourteen. Linn Harwell's mother had had five children, eight pregnancies. Gwen Elliott's mother had two small children and had just separated from her husband. Their reasons died with them. What lived on were their motherless children.

"My father said that when they took me to the cemetery somebody told me she was sleeping," says Commander Elliott, "and I thought that anytime he wanted he could go get her. My father says I used to ask 'Why don't we go get Mommy?' but I don't remember it."

That is the shadow of things to come.

AT THE CLINICS

April 5, 1992

Last fall a thirty-year-old woman named Eileen Moran pulled into
the parking lot of the Aware Woman clinic in the space coast
town of Melbourne, Florida. Ms. Moran was not surprised to see
demonstrators; that is commonplace. The surprise came the next
day, in a manila envelope full of color photographs of bloody
fetuses, anti-abortion tracts, and a letter warning her about procedures performed at the clinic.

"I felt very violated," says Ms. Moran, who is now five months
pregnant and had gone to the clinic only for a checkup. "The
idea that they could trace my name and address through my
license plate and have something in the mail that day was pretty
terrifying."

At Aware Woman, it is pretty ordinary. Ms. Moran got off easier
than the teenager whose envelope was sent to her parents. And
her experience pales in comparison to that of doctors who
receive middle-of-the-night hang-up calls on their unlisted lines
and whose homes are picketed constantly. Opponents of the Mel-

bourne clinic have issued WANTED posters, offering a $1,000 reward for information leading to "the arrest or conviction" of one doctor who works there.

The poster, which describes him as "a hired assassin in that he kills unborn babies for a fee," includes his photograph, his home phone number and that of his mother, and the license-plate number of his car. The poster was taped to the office doors of other gynecologists in central Florida; written at the bottom was "You Are Next."

Today in Washington, D.C., there will be a rally for abortion rights, for constitutional protections and federal legislation. But while we have been looking at the big picture we have forgotten something important. What if they gave us abortion and nobody came—no doctors, no clinic administrators, no nurses?

The people who run abortion clinics are a tightly knit group, as folks who are under fire tend to be. Their carpenters have been persuaded not to make repairs, their medical labs to turn away their business. Their children have been accosted and told that they are the spawn of murderers. I couldn't blame any of them if they decided that they'd had enough of being the real people behind the legal arguments.

You can find the place where the founder of the Melbourne clinic lives because there is a groove in the grass out front, where every morning a woman walks back and forth with a sign that says PAT WINDLE, STOP KILLING GOD'S BABIES.

Few new doctors are learning to perform abortions, and those who do, concerned that publicity like the WANTED posters will ruin their practices, often return to the happier task of delivering babies. The big medical organizations, which can lobby like nobody's business when they want to, have been uncommonly low-key. They were more fired up about our right to choose breast implants than they have ever been about our right to choose abortion.

Ms. Windle says that a reporter scoffed when she described this as a civil war. But it is a war, and there is battle fatigue. There has sprung up a thirst for some middle ground. Sometimes the talk is of promoting contraception, sometimes of curtailing the period of pregnancy during which abortion is permissible, sometimes of merely allowing abortion while making clear that it is not desirable.

But this battle is not being driven by those with a will to compromise. The people who are harassing doctors, patients, and clinics consider any means permissible in their quest to prove that they know what's better for you than you do. The ordinary American standards of personal privacy and personal property don't apply. "God's law is higher than man's law," says Randall Terry, the leader of Operation Rescue, who said in Buffalo that he would be using investigators to dig up dirt on doctors who perform abortions, a part of God's law that I missed in my study of the Bible.

And so it is important today to remember a T-shirt slogan: Think Globally, Act Locally. Many of us who speak out in favor of legal abortion have had little to do with the day-to-day happenings at the clinics, perhaps because we were focused on sweeping safeguards, perhaps because it is easier to see abortion as a crusade than as a business. The truth is it must be both. Freedom of the press is only as meaningful as the willingness of one person to publish a newspaper. The right to choose abortion is empty if the people who provide it are harassed out of existence.

HEARTS AND
MINDS

April 22, 1992

Today the Supreme Court will hear arguments on a Pennsylvania law that would restrict access to abortion in that state. Today demonstrators from both sides of the question will face each other across the unbridgeable moat of their disparate beliefs outside clinics in Buffalo.

What about tomorrow?

With all this activity, in the courts and in the streets, it is important to remember that we have taken this debate exactly nowhere in the last twenty years. The great social issues of this country are settled not with placards or legal briefs finally but in hearts and minds. While the standard-bearers on both sides posit from the margins of perfect certainty, the great majority learn nothing that they didn't already know about abortion.

There has been a lot of talk that the Pennsylvania statute is a kind of abortion-rights Armageddon. It includes parental consent and spousal notification, a twenty-four-hour waiting period and medical counseling about other available options, the procedure, and the gestational age of the fetus.

I do not like this law. It has as its subtext the assumption, prevalent among anti-abortion zealots, that women decide to have abortions in the same way they decide to have manicures. But it does not serve our credibility to inflate its provisions. When we squander our rhetoric on restrictions in Pennsylvania, what does that leave us for the law in Louisiana, a slam-dunk of legal abortion that allows it only in limited cases of rape and incest or to save the life of the mother?

More important, when we excoriate waiting periods and parental consent we dismiss the ambivalence of many Americans and we miss an opportunity to communicate beyond the slogans. Waiting periods sound reasonable—until you evoke the impoverished mother of three who has driven six hundred miles and has only one day's worth of baby-sitting money in her pocket.

Parental consent is constantly justified with the aspirin analogy, the idea that a girl who cannot get Tylenol in school without a parent's permission should not be able to have an abortion without that permission. That's because the judicial bypass that is a required alternative to consent is little more than a phrase. You have only to describe a fifteen-year-old pleading her case before a judge to make some people understand that this alleged attempt to legislate communication is designed to intimidate instead.

The spousal notification provision is supposed to send the message that husbands have rights, too. But common sense tells us all that a woman who can't discuss this with her husband probably has a reason so potent that no law is going to deter her.

In short, there are many talking points. It is simply that we have not talked. We have taken stands, and stood.

I understand the positioning that is taking place here, to drum up support by evoking an imminent threat to legal abortion. And I understand the frustration at an issue that it seems will never be settled, and the temptation to meet zealotry with zealotry.

But it saddens me to see some of those who support abortion

rights in Buffalo using language as ugly as that of the people who send me anonymous postcards filled with vitriol and photographs of fetuses. I imagined we were better than that. I picture folks seeing this on television and thinking that both groups are lousy with lunatics.

Most Americans, the polls tell us, feel truly represented by neither side. They are the people who say they simultaneously believe abortion is wrong and it is a private matter. While the demonstrators see black and white, they see gray.

In 1990, Archbishop Rembert G. Weakland of Milwaukee held six "listening sessions" to hear what Catholic women were saying about abortion. I wish in every town in America someone would do what the honorable archbishop did: bring people together to talk, to disagree, and above all to acknowledge the gray areas.

If we rely on elections and legislation, those of us who believe abortion should be legal, our fortunes will vary with the personnel. If we make people feel their ambivalence is unacceptable, then we've lost them. But if we have reached out to, and reached, the hearts and minds of average Americans with honest discussion, that will drive so much of the rest.

Or we can continue moving from legal argument to legal argument, confrontation to confrontation, as we will today.

But what about tomorrow?

ONE VOTE

July 1, 1992

History was being made Monday. You could tell because Harry Blackmun and Randall Terry agreed about something. Justice Blackmun, the author of *Roe* v. *Wade,* and Mr. Terry, the founder of Operation Rescue, both said the same thing when the Supreme Court decision affirming a constitutional right to abortion but upholding state restrictions was handed down.

One vote, they each said, one with anguish, the other with rage. One vote.

That is what you need to remember about what happened this week. The ruling on *Roe* was 5 to 4. One vote. It was a most confusing day. It is not often that those who support legal abortion and those who oppose it agree on anything. But both said the decision was dreadful, and that left many Americans befuddled about what it all meant.

It was a most personal ruling by the Court, as though the tumult in the streets was a fever that had reached inside and infected even those nine so insulated from the world.

Justice Scalia's dissent espousing the overthrow of *Roe* was angry and dismissive of the majority opinion. "Its length, and what might be called its epic tone, suggest that its authors believe they are bringing to an end a troublesome era," he sniped.

Justice Blackmun's frustration at the ebb tide of judicial liberalism burst out in an attack on Chief Justice Rehnquist: "The chief justice's criticism of *Roe* follows from his stunted conception of individual liberty."

But perhaps the most personal part of the decision was that upholding the right to an abortion. Written by Justices Souter, Kennedy, and O'Connor, characterized by Justice Blackmun as "an act of personal courage," it stated a central truth, too seldom evoked: "the liberty of the woman is at stake in a sense unique to the human condition and so unique to the law."

And it continued: "The mother who carries a child to full term is subject to anxieties, to physical constraints, to pain that only she must bear. That these sacrifices have from the beginning of the human race been endured by woman with a pride that ennobles her in the eyes of others and gives to the infant a bond of love cannot alone be grounds for the state to insist she make the sacrifice.

"Her suffering is too intimate and personal for the state to insist, without more, upon its own vision of the woman's role, however dominant that vision has been in the course of our history and our culture. The destiny of the woman must be shaped to a large extent on her own conception of her spiritual imperatives and her place in society."

Those leaders with whom I agree about the necessity of legal abortion concentrated not upon the eloquent vision in that opinion but upon the restrictions upheld. I think waiting periods make abortion unnecessarily difficult for women who must travel great distances, and parental consent is intended to scare teenagers who must face a judge if they cannot face their mothers. I mourn a shift from a "fundamental right" to a right which must only contain no "undue burden."

But it does not serve accurate reporting—or even successful spin control—to say this decision guts *Roe*. Quite the contrary: justices once thought hostile to the unique questions of liberty and privacy raised by this issue apprehend them in ways we did not imagine. They got it, folks. And I, for one, applaud.

I am sorry the Pennsylvania restrictions were upheld. But today it is critical to stress the reaffirmation and how tenuously it holds. If we want to raise the alarm, it will not be done by decrying counseling provisions.

Justice Blackmun: "I fear for the darkness as four justices anxiously await the single vote necessary to extinguish the light."

Mr. Terry: "We need one more justice. . . ."

George Bush has shown himself willing to nominate a second-rate jurist to satisfy a standard of conservative extremism. And zealots like Mr. Terry will be pressuring him for another such. "I am 83 years old," Justice Blackmun wrote plaintively of his mortality and perhaps of *Roe*'s. Surely this must shape the election. Surely Republican women must consider how they will explain to their daughters their reelection of a man who will attempt to rescind the basic human right of bodily integrity.

One vote. Pennsylvania is important. November is critical. This has always been a personal matter. It just got more personal. One vote. Yours.

THE TRUTH
TELLING

July 5, 1992

When she wrote about a Supreme Court decision on the liability of tobacco companies, *New York Times* reporter Linda Greenhouse included a paragraph, part human interest, part factoid, explaining which of the justices smoked.

She was in no position to do something along the same lines last week when the Court handed down its decision on abortion. There was no obvious way of telling if anyone on the Court had family or friends who had once ended a pregnancy.

That is because abortion is considered a most private act. Many women have never told their parents, their children, or even their friends. They live closeted in this respect.

It is a truism that the more we apprehend the world personally, the more empathetically we respond to it. One of the reasons homophobia has eased a bit is that more and more of us know gay people as friends, as colleagues, as sisters and brothers. That is because more of them are open about who they are. The openness and the understanding feed on each other, in a kind of circular argument of familiarity that breeds not contempt but knowledge.

In the introduction to *The Choices We Made,* a book of personal accounts of abortion, Gloria Steinem wrote: "From the prisoners whose stories started the storming of the Bastille and the French revolution to the 'speaking bitterness' groups of China, from the church 'testifying' that started the civil rights movement to the consciousness-raising that began this most recent wave of feminism, populist truth telling has been the heart and soul of movements and revolutions all over the world."

Ms. Steinem herself was part of the truth telling when she and other prominent American women, including Lillian Hellman, Susan Sontag, Nora Ephron, Barbara Tuchman, and Billie Jean King, signed a manifesto in the first issue of *Ms.* magazine witnessing to their own abortions, a "campaign for honesty and freedom."

That was twenty years ago, twenty years during which close to 30 million abortions were performed in the United States. It is difficult to believe you do not know someone who has had one. Or perhaps you simply do not know you know. One of the ironies of parental-notification legislation is that the world demands sixteen-year-olds to tell their parents about their abortions when it is filled with forty-year-olds who have never done so.

What Gloria Steinem and the other women who joined her did in 1972 was courageous. But, like listening to Cybill Shepherd rue a bad marriage, it may have seemed removed from everyday experience. We feel that the prominent are somehow different.

In the minds of so many ordinary people, the women who have abortions are different, too, not quite like them. Perhaps that will continue until the day someone turns and says, "Mom, Dad, I have something important to tell you about my life." Or until the woman at the next desk, hearing for the umpteenth time about how maybe it ought to be legal but Lord, I could never do it myself, finally blurts out, "Oh yes you could. I did."

It is easier to be judgmental about a construct than about a friend.

I oppose outing. I don't believe any gay man or lesbian, no matter how prominent, should be forced to retire privacy for the good of the cause, although I believe openness does the cause good. And I believe the only person entitled to know whether or not any woman has had an abortion is the woman herself.

But when I hear people talk about abortions of convenience and abortion on demand, I know there is one superlative way to counter those utterly misleading modifiers. That is by testifying, bearing witness, truth telling. That's how you learn what this really means, not by statistics or demonstrations or even court opinions. And it's why, millions of abortions later, many Americans still don't understand how central this liberty is to so many lives. No one has leaned across the kitchen table and told them.

We moved forward last week, with a reaffirmation of the constitutional right to choose abortion that was as much about women as it was about issues. That is the stereotype that silence reinforces—that this is an issue. It is millions of stories, each one different. Many of them you know—sister, daughter, friend—except perhaps for the silence in the center where the abortion was. Silence is our right, too. But it sometimes leaves truth untold.

NO MORE WAITING

July 22, 1992

From time to time you hear complaints from people of apparent goodwill about how much national attention is being focused on AIDS. What about cancer? say cancer survivors. What about heart disease? And in these complaints there is usually a touch of envy. Many of us whose lives were mangled by mortal illnesses suffered privately, confident that doctors and researchers and the purveyors of government grants were doing their level best to eradicate the scourge. We waited. And waited. And waited.

Then the AIDS activists disrupted hearings and marched down city streets and agitated, agitated, agitated for better drugs, for speedier approvals, for more research money. Some people think they are too militant. If I could help give someone I loved a second chance, or even an extra year, what people think would not worry me a bit.

It's certain that we women can learn from this, after all these years of waiting politely for a male medical and governmental establishment to be nice to us. When the president pandered yet again to the anti-abortion lobby by vetoing a measure that would pay for research on women's health issues because it also lifted the ban on fetal-tissue research, it was clear we'd been polite too long.

And then there's RU-486, a pill that causes early abortion. Comparisons are odious, but imagine if doctors discovered a method of vasectomy that required only a handful of capsules and a drink of water. It'd be approved so fast it would make your head spin.

A pregnant social worker named Leona Benten was stopped at Kennedy Airport when she flew in from Europe carrying a duly prescribed dose of RU-486. The drug is on a special import alert list, although even some Food and Drug Administration officials say that this has nothing to do with safety. It didn't go on the list at the behest of serious scientists, but at the request of conservative members of Congress, thereby making the F.D.A. an arm of the right-to-life lobby.

But RU-486 is not just a drug that induces abortion. There is evidence that it may help fight breast cancer, a disease that leads to the deaths of forty-four thousand American women a year. Some doctors think the drug could prove useful in treating adult diabetes, hypertension, and other cancers. But they—and you, if you suffer from any of those conditions—are stymied here in the United States by the unhappy alliance of politics, medicine, and corporate caution.

The manufacturers of RU-486, Roussel Uclaf, have acted as businesses tend to do. They pulled it off the market in their native France after there were protests, putting it back on only after the French government ordered them to do so. They will not even apply for a license in this country, where posses of men illustrate their respect for life by thrusting fetal remains at candidates and clinic escorts. In several European countries, where there is less fetus throwing, RU-486 is being used with success and safety.

There is a kind of resonance to all this for anyone who has

read Ellen Chesler's marvelous biography of Margaret Sanger. One legal challenge described in the book is entitled—truly— *United States* v. *One Package Containing 120, more or less, Rubber Pessaries to Prevent Conception.* The offending devices were sent to Mrs. Sanger by a Japanese doctor, then confiscated by customs. This was not an uncommon problem; after Mrs. Sanger married the inventor of 3-in-One oil, he smuggled diaphragms in the product's containers. It all seems rather quaint, as Leona Benten's difficulties will someday, which is cold comfort to her today.

Ms. Benten brought the ban on RU-486 to the public's attention. Sadly, the attendant fuss may also have reinforced Roussef Uclaf's dedication to conflict avoidance in the United States, at least for the time being.

But contained in this episode are the seeds of a powerful lobby: women who want abortions to be performed as early and as safely as possible; women who have lost mothers to breast cancer and are at risk themselves; women who believe that health care should be separate from a political agenda.

Oh, and women who vote. Those familiar with the politics of RU-486 believe that it could be licensed in short order if the political atmosphere changed. Not in time for Leona Benten, but not a moment too soon for millions of other women who must be less patient and more militant about health care.

BEARS WITH
FURNITURE

October 18, 1990

Some of the best comedians right now are women, and the best of the women comedians is named Rita Rudner. She does great bits on men, and in one of them she says: "Men don't live well by themselves. They don't even live like people. They live like bears with furniture."

I always wondered about that furniture part.

Since the observations of female comedians, women lawyers, my aunt Gloria, the entire membership of the Hadassah, the League of Women Voters nationwide, and the woman who lives across the street from me don't count as empirical evidence, researchers at the University of California at San Francisco have done a study that shows that men need to be married or they starve to death. They studied 7,651 American adults to come to this conclusion.

This is why we think scientists are wasting their research money. This study says that men between the ages of forty-five and sixty-five who live alone or with somebody other than a wife are twice as likely to die within ten years as men of the same age who live with their wives. "The critical factor seems to be the spouse," said a professor of epidemiology and biostatistics who, incredibly enough, seems both to be surprised by these findings and to be female. She also noted that researchers were not sure why men without wives are in danger of an earlier death, but that preliminary analysis suggested they ate poorly.

Let me explain how you might do a study like this. Let's say you have a package of Stouffer's macaroni and cheese, a tomato, and a loaf of French bread. Let's say that it is seven o'clock. Pretend you are a researcher for the University of California and observe what the woman between the ages of forty-five and sixty-four will do with these materials:

1) Preheats oven according to package directions. Puts package in oven.

2) Slices tomato and sprinkles with oil, vinegar, and ground pepper.

3) Slices bread and removes butter from refrigerator.

In about an hour the woman will eat.

At the same time researchers can observe a man between the ages of forty-five and sixty-four living alone using the same materials:

1) Reads package, peers at stove, rereads package, reads financial section of paper.

2) Looks at tomato, says aloud, "Where the hell's the knife?"

3) Places tomato on top of frozen package, leaves both on kitchen counter, watches *Monday Night Football* or a National Geographic documentary on the great horned owl while eating a loaf of unsliced French bread.

This can be compared and contrasted with the man living with his wife. When the wife goes out, the result is exactly the same as in example 2, except that when the wife returns and says, "Why didn't you eat dinner?" the husband between the ages of forty-five and sixty-four will say, "I wasn't hungry," in exactly the same tone of voice he would use if he were to say, "I have bubonic plague."

(These results are occasionally skewed by observed occasions on which wife returns home and finds house full of smoke. Such incidents are particularly reliable indicators of longer life for men between the ages of forty-five and sixty-four, since they enhance the well-documented "I told you not to go out and leave me alone" effect, which promotes a generalized feeling of well-being and smugness.)

Every woman I know finds the California study notable only because the results seem so obvious. But I find it helpful to have anecdotal observations confirmed by scientific analysis, and besides, it gets me off the hook. I am frequently accused of feminist bias for suggesting that the ability to do a simple household task without talking about it for weeks is gender-based.

If I were to suggest that a man without a wife is a man overwhelmed by dust balls, pizza cartons, and mortality, I would get an earful from the New Age men. The New Age men appear in many stories about life-style matters; there are five of them, and they are the guys who actually took those paternity leaves you've been hearing so much about. One of them makes a mean veal piccata, which is habitually featured in stories about men who cook.

If they're unhappy with this conclusion, they've got science to arm-wrestle with. $E = MC^2$, some guy once said, perhaps while eating a loaf of French bread and wondering why his wife had to visit her sister. And 1 man minus 1 wife – bad news, according to researchers at the University of California at San Francisco. Bears with furniture. Rita and I have biostatistics on our side.

DIRT AND DIGNITY

July 22, 1990

She walked into the courtroom, which was an accomplishment all by itself. "She looked great," said one observer, "for a person who's been beaten to death." By the time she testified, wearing a purple suit and assorted scars, it had become almost fitting that the only thing we did not know about her was her name.

She has taken on mythic proportions, this woman who was found with more of her blood on the ground than in her body, whose face was shattered like a china cup. Her survival became a resurrection, and she became an archetype: the Central Park jogger. And the trial of the teenagers accused of her destruction is a microcosm of city living at its worst: sordid, mean, racially charged. The proceedings are reminiscent of the crime. There is dirt everywhere.

The jury has seen videotapes that detail a night of *Clockwork Orange* adolescent fun: beating up a vagrant, chasing bicyclists, gang raping an investment banker. Videotape is the prosecutor's friend. You can see with your own eyes that no one is holding sixteen-year-old Antron McCray down as he talks, that his face is not bleeding, that his answers are not punctuated with a love tap from a billy club.

Instead, he sits with his parents at his elbow, looking like every kid called on the carpet in the principal's office, fidgety as he talks about kicking, grabbing, climbing on top. His mother and father let him talk to the police. This is the mistake parents make at precinct houses. They let their children talk when any good defense attorney would tell them to keep their mouths shut. Without a confession, there would have been no case here. With a confession, there is only coercion as a defense.

The defense says the confessions were coerced. It has also suggested that there was no rape. Some supporters of the defendants have suggested even worse than that. They talk in the corridors of the courthouse about how this is a racist frame-up against the black teenagers, about how the investment banker jogged north in the park to buy drugs or to seek exactly the kind of trouble she found. They see nothing perverse in the suggestion that a woman would want to be hunted down and torn apart. They call her filthy names.

Even prosecutors had a piece of the victimization. Forensics have failed them. To show that a rape was committed, the prosecutor asked the victim about her sex life, about her method of birth control, about whether she was wearing the same jogging pants she had worn the last time she had sex with her boyfriend. We do not print her name, but we know that she used a diaphragm. You have to wonder about women out there, recently raped, still undecided about going to the police, reading all this and thinking, "Forget it. Not me."

Only one person has emerged from this mess pristine in the public eye, and ironically it is the person who is best known covered with blood and mud, whose white running shirt was stained that rusty brown that shouts "evidence." With most horrific crimes we remember the criminals. Richard Speck. David Berkowitz. The Boston Strangler. In this crime, everyone thinks first of the victim. She had all the best things—the right schools, the Phi Beta Kappa key, the fast-track job, the athlete's discipline and devotion to her running—until the moment when her life became defined by one of the worst things that could happen to a human being.

She refused to die. By most medical standards, the charge in this case should have been murder. The doctors said that perhaps her will saved her, the same will that powered her running and twelve-hour workdays. For years we have been wondering what the point is to lives that lead us like carrots on a stick always a little ahead of our noses. Here was an answer. You could use the energy to save your own life.

She has not sold her story to a supermarket tabloid, and she has not made a jeans commercial. Her mother turns away interviewers with a dignified demurral: "We are united in our silence." The silence was broken for twelve minutes. There was no cross-examination. This was the smartest thing the defense has done so far.

It would have been easy to cry about the double vision, the loss of balance, the month she can't remember, the people who did this. But she didn't cry. She took the witness stand, and then she left. Maybe she ran that evening. In a city that can turn a person into a celebrity overnight, she has become that strangest of things, a celebrity nobody knows. And she has become New York rising above the dirt, the New Yorker who has known the best, and the worst, and has stayed on, living somewhere in the middle.

THE CEMENT FLOOR

August 28, 1991

Women prospered cute in the 1980s. Every time you turned around, there was some cute story about a woman high school quarterback, a woman sanitation worker, or a woman hard hat.

Eventually, after the sideshows were over, real life went on. Women were admitted where their talents could take them, and their talents took them far. There were more women in all walks of life, many of them places from which you could draw a decent paycheck.

This makes equal opportunity sound simple, and it never has been. There emerged a plateau for women on their way up, between the push of progress and the peak of the male hierarchy. This week the Feminist Majority Foundation released a report saying that less than 3 percent of the corporate officers at the country's biggest companies are female. There seems to be an invisible barrier to the ascension of women, a barrier we call the glass ceiling.

There are also cement floors.

Until recently Teresa Cox was a baseball umpire and, by most accounts, a very good one. Women umpires refused to be novelty acts. Pam Postema, the best known, once said of players' taunts, "If you're black, they key on that; if you're fat, they say you're too fat to see the play. And if they insult you personally, and keep it up, that constitutes abuse, and you throw them out." Nice matter-of-fact attitude. It didn't do Ms. Postema any good; she was let go in 1989.

During the 1980s, four women umpired in the minor leagues. None ever made it to the majors. Ms. Cox, the latest to be thrown out, will argue the call. She is suing, saying that the good old boys who run umpiring have decided women don't belong, no matter how able. I can't tell you what the good old boys say, because their good old representative refused to talk.

But I have some sense of the other side from Harry Wendelstadt, the veteran umpire who trained Teresa Cox and calls her "the best female candidate I've ever had." He says he's trained twenty-eight women and maybe five thousand men, and that there just haven't been enough women in the pipeline leading to the major leagues. That's what we hear about the executive suite, too—that it's a pipeline problem.

"I don't think there's bias," Mr. Wendelstadt says. "I have no doubt that someday there'll be a woman umpire in the major leagues; I just hope I'm the one who trains her." Mr. Wendelstadt sounds O.K. and then he misses a high hanging curveball; he adds, "I don't know why a young lady would want this job." They should have this line printed on a T-shirt for men in traditionally male fields, they say it so often. Why does anyone want any job? Because it's suited to her skills, well paying, interesting. Because it's there. Hormones have nothing to do with wanting to feed your family or use your talents.

Teresa Cox says that when she first started calling strikes, she was told that her voice was too high, and that when she used a lower register, she was criticized for sounding phony. She says she was told the umpire uniform looked awkward on women; I've seen guys wearing it who look as if they're in the third trimester. She says that a league supervisor wondered aloud whether she was "queer." She also says she was told she didn't need the job because she'd just get married and have kids.

Now, that's an original line.

"She was told by the supervisors that women in baseball were just a joke," says Glenda Cochran, her lawyer.

Mr. Wendelstadt says it must be that she wasn't quite good enough, and in fact we've all heard of cases in which women cried sexism when the problem was skill. I always think that's a little like faking sick with the flu; you can get away with it because there's so much of the real thing going around.

The glass ceiling gets more attention, but it's good to remember the cement floor, to remember that there are still places that might as well have signs: GIRLS KEEP OUT! It serves to remind you of the bad old days, and of the fact that there's nothing cute about trying to be treated fairly. Why would a young lady want this job? You'll just get married and have kids! The reservations are couched more subtly now, but they're there, like Burma-Shave signs along the highway of equal opportunity. What a long, strange trip it's been. Some wins. Some losses. Some places where we just keep striking out.

A TEAM DREAM

July 8, 1992

People talk about turning forty as though it were akin to having your wisdom teeth removed—exceedingly painful, the horrid loss of something grown in the bone. The loss of that gilded age called youth, which is wasted on the young and which many grown-ups wouldn't have on a bet, knowing what they know today.

So far, Day One, forty feels fine. The days of expensive fashion errors, crazed momentary friendships, and 2:00 A.M. feedings are over. Things are somehow settled. There are those who think settled is synonymous with death and stagnation; I'm the kind who thinks settled is synonymous with security.

"It is in the thirties that we want friends," F. Scott Fitzgerald wrote. "In the forties we know they won't save us any more than love did." This adds to my collection of things Fitzgerald said that are foolish. If not friendship and love, then what? Insider trading? The real wisdom comes from George Burns, who once said of growing old, "Consider the alternative." Consider the alternative. There you are. The only real regret I feel today is that I am not a member of the United States Olympic men's basketball team. No, this is not a woman/jock/empowerment fantasy, and no, I haven't yet seen *A League of Their Own*. That's women and baseball, and I don't ever have to write about baseball.

Somewhere in the contract of the male columnist it is written that once a year he must wax poetic and philosophic about baseball, making it sound like a cross between the Kirov and Zen Buddhism. This covers the baseball profundity axis more than adequately, which is a good thing. The connection between a base hit and karma eludes me.

But basketball is something different, sweatier and swifter and not likely to be likened to haiku, thank God. And this Olympic basketball team is something different entirely. It is the best sports team ever, the equivalent of rounding up the greatest American writers of the last century or so and watching them collaborate: "O.K., Twain, you do the dialogue and hand off to Faulkner. He'll do the interior monlogue. Hemingway will edit— no, don't make that face, you know you overwrite. And be nice to Cheever. He's young, but he's got a good ear. Wharton and Cather can't play—they're girls." On television they were running down the lineup: Larry Bird. Patrick Ewing. Michael Jordan. Magic Johnson. When they got to Christian Laettner, the student prince of college basektball, I almost felt sorry for the guy because he was so outclassed, a mere champion among giants. We don't see giants often, even one at a time, never mind en masse and in skivvies.

Catholic school girls once played intramural basketball all winter long, and though it was with a smaller ball and slacker rules than the boys used—and though I traveled more often than I ever scored—it gave me a visceral feeling for the nonpareil grace, skill, and teamwork of the sport. Not to mention that glow in your chest when the ball leaves your hands, arcs through the air with all eyes following, and falls almost inevitably through the hoop. Yesssss.

Take all that and elevate it to the level of, say, Frank Lloyd Wright, and you have this Olympic team. As good as it gets. There is pure pleasure in thinking about watching them play together. Each is accustomed to being a star; together they're a firmament. The collaboration is one of the loveliest parts, a metaphor for the friendship whose salvation Fitzgerald so mistakenly denied.

Twenty years ago I wouldn't have noticed. I liked the figure skaters then, all sequins and spins and solitary splendor, the girls who epitomize the Victorian dictum that men perspire and women glow. I've lost my yen for sequins and developed a pure reverence for skill and sweat.

Those guys won't be out there getting rich or famous; they're already rich and famous. Every lay-up, every rebound in Barcelona will be saying, "Look at what we know." Not youth, youth, youth, although some of them are very young. Experience. There's a moment when the ball arcs perfectly downward to the waiting web of the net—or when the words lie down just right on the page—that makes you feel as if you are going to live forever. The irony is that by the time you are old enough to appreciate the feeling, you're old enough to know that it's illusory. Experience. Experience. I never had a jump shot, and I'm no longer a kid. But experience I now have. Consider the alternative.

HEROINE
ADDICTION

April 29, 1990

Quick—who is Jo March?

I've been taking an unscientific survey. The results: not a single man I know—and we're talking educated men here—has had the faintest idea. One guessed that Jo March was a second baseman for the Baltimore Orioles.

Every woman I asked got it right. They were a skewed sample, to be sure, the intellectual, the ambitious, even the driven. And every one knew Jo March of *Little Women*, a boyish girl who can never keep her hair up or her gloves clean, who thinks social niceties are a waste of time and spends her happiest hours in the attic plugging away at her writing.

Meg is domestic, Beth sweet and sickly, and Amy is pretty and marries the boy who loved Jo first. Jo is the smart one, and that is why she left an indelible mark. She showed that there was more to life than spinning skeins into gold and marrying a prince.

There weren't many little women like that in the books we read as girls. Nancy Drew was kind of a wimp. I liked Madeline—"To the tiger in the zoo/Madeline just said, 'Pooh-pooh'"—and Anne of Green Gables. As I grew older, I began to hope that there would be real women to replace the fictional ones, that out there were strong, determined human beings of my own sex.

On the short list of those women, I always placed Simone de Beauvoir near the top.

I was not alone. At the women's college I attended it was difficult to find a reading list without *The Second Sex*, that powerful and uncompromising feminist manifesto. Ten years ago, when Deirdre Bair found the lives of women in a jumble because of the competing interests of work, family, and ego, she decided to do a biography of de Beauvoir, that woman whose life seemed to epitomize freedom.

The recently published result is a fine, fine book, and about as depressing a thing as I've read since the end of *Little Women*, when Jo inexplicably marries some codger who lives in a rooming house.

It is not that you cannot relate to the great French feminist philosopher. The problem is that women can relate only too well. There was the father who was thrilled that she thought like a man. There was the examining committee torn between giving first place to her or to a male student, finally deciding on him because he was taking his exams for the second time.

And there was that other student himself. His name was Jean-Paul Sartre, and he became a great philosopher. He and de Beauvoir never married, and they have always seemed an example of one of the great egalitarian relationships.

Ha! It was always his comfort that came first. She stooped when she was with him so he wouldn't seem so short. She brought him leather-bound books in which to write and then used cheap children's exercise paper for her own work.

Whole sections of the book could be the basis for telephone calls between one smart woman and another over the behavior of a third: "Wait till you hear what that creep has done to her now!" In Sartre's case, as in so many of such telephone calls, the behavior was tediously predictable: when he wasn't practicing the yo-yo or producing brilliant work, he slept with women, many of them women Simone brought home. She said it wasn't important.

The book could be subtitled as self-help: *Smart Woman, Idiotic Choices, or What I Did for Love.*

Lo, how the Valkyrie has fallen. She sublimated her work to his. "He was so superior," she told Ms. Bair. "You don't understand what we had." She sounds like every woman who thinks some guy is going to give definition to her life. She gave definition to my life by writing *The Second Sex*, a book that made me feel it could be fine to be female.

"I thought if I could just find a woman who made it all work it would help me and everyone else," says Ms. Bair. "I thought I had found the ideal woman. But she was a real person, like all the rest of us."

We don't want real people. We want giants. And the disfranchised want them perfect because we have so few. Perhaps this is one reason African-Americans were unhappy about material in the Ralph David Abernathy book—not news, certainly—on Martin Luther King's infidelity. I suspect it is why feminists are unhappy with Deirdre Bair.

Do as I say, not as I do—that is one lesson of de Beauvoir's life. But nothing she did can minimize what she said, that women deserve freedom. She learned the lesson partly from one of the most important fictional characters of her childhood, Jo March.

"I think that somehow even when very young," de Beauvoir said, "I must have perceived that Jo was always making choices and sometimes they were neither well reasoned nor good. The idea of choice must have frightened me a little, but it was exhilarating as well."

\\\\\\

REBELS WITHOUT
A CLUE

September 18, 1991

At the beginning of each new season, fashion designers provide a great service for the women of America. They make them laugh.

They do not rely simply on their prices. Each season they supplement sticker shock with some new concept that is sure to amuse anyone leading a reality-based life. Several years ago they made evening dresses with big puffy skirts that rose below your chin like taffeta goiters when you sat down, and this spring a few of them had a bad attack of fuchsia and chartreuse, apparently unaware that women do not want to look like toucans.

Then there are sad retailing stories that no one is buying clothes. That's because the emperors are designing them.

For fall they've outdone themselves. "This season you can be sure there will be a zippered leather jacket and a tartan pleated skirt in your fashion future," the fashion column said yesterday.

I'm sure.

When I realized that the fashion future was going to be Terminator chic with parochial-school overtones, I had to remind myself that fashion is not about clothes. I was going to say it is about the way we see ourselves, but that's not true either. It's about the way people with perfumes named after them see themselves.

Calvin Klein, for example, has paid a great deal of money for a little magazine that came packaged with *Vanity Fair*. It consists of photographs that have something to do with rock concerts, something to do with motorcycles (I feel a theme developing here), something to do with naked men, and a good deal to do with sex. It is said to be an advertisement for jeans and must have something to do with how Calvin Klein sees himself, sort of like a surreal high school yearbook for a grown man.

Designer motorcycle jackets might mean designers see women as strong, adventurous people who take no nonsense. Or they might mean that designers see us as a lean, mean coven of empowered witches roaring in to try to mow men down.

Or they might signal a massive identity crisis, a backlash from the gimme-gimme eighties. Chanel has made some of its suits this season in denim, and the couture house filled the windows of Bergdorf Goodman with Harley-Davidsons and mannequins wearing biker boots, megabucks organza, and what someone at the store describes as "authentic Marlon Brando motorcycle caps." The message is clear: Déclassé! Danger! Divine!

The kindest possible thing you can say about this is that it is an affectation. The motorcycle jackets may have one saving grace, and that is that it is difficult to imagine someone approaching you on the street to hiss, "How many cows died to make that coat?"

Perhaps some designers are inspired by Madonna. But they must remember the difference between the business meetings of Madonna and the business meetings of the rest of us.

Woman named Madonna: I want $3 million.

Male authority figure: Fine.

As opposed to:

Woman named something else: Your Honor, I'd like to approach the bench.

Male authority figure: Why?

Woman: I represent the defendant, Your Honor.

Male authority figure: In that ridiculous motorcycle jacket, I thought you were the defendant.

The thing to remember is that high fashion has little to do with what women wear and a lot to do with what retailers mark down later. Occasionally they get it right. Many of us would like to shake hands with the designer of the elasticized waist or the person who resurrected flat shoes. And some mistakes were our own. There were those suits with the neck thing like a dead pocket handkerchief that almost killed feminism.

There remains a gender gap between men's clothes, which have been the same since the pharaohs shopped Brooks Brothers, and women's clothes, which date even as they hang on store racks. Some men therefore find women's clothes confusing, except for short skirts and anything strapless, which they find completely understandable.

Here is all anyone needs to know about this fall: leather motorcycle jackets and plaid pleated skirts. On models. And on the racks that say SALE PRICED in January.

GETTING A SECOND WIND

February 23, 1992

Desiree Washington says somebody offered to pay her off. She told this to Barbara Walters on national television Friday night. Ms. Washington is sweet and earnest, the kind of young woman who would have shown up at a train station with a small valise, big eyes, and high hopes in old-fashioned movie musicals if old-fashioned movie musicals ever cast black people. She is the woman who was raped by Mike Tyson.

She says she was offered a million dollars to drop the charges, which is an awful lot of money to offer someone if you think they're lying. The matter's under investigation, so she wouldn't name names. But she says the people who offered her money also offered her names to say, magic words to explain to the public why she was loath to go forward.

Patricia Bowman. Anita Hill.

She didn't budge.

It's been a great time for women in America. I know that conclusion seems contrary to fact. The reason many were shocked that Mike Tyson was convicted was not because they thought he was innocent. Quite the contrary. It was that for the last year being female in America seemed like a bad country-western song: "Can't Win for Losing."

It wasn't only, for example, that Dow Corning had manufactured a product of questionable safety after questionable research. It was that the suits who run the company were dismissive of women who complained about their breast implants. In this way, they deftly turned what might have been handled as a public relations problem into the national nightmare they richly deserve. They were cold and closed-minded when openness and compassion were called for. They treated their consumers like crybabies. They didn't take them seriously.

That is why it's been a good year—because we've taken ourselves seriously. Any good reporter knows that the best way to illuminate an issue is to write about the people who embody it. It's been more than two decades since the world began to change so dramatically for women, but this revolution has been long on issues and short on people to embody them.

When Barnard College asked its entering freshman class to list the women they most admired, Eleanor Roosevelt led the pack. Among the living, Margaret Thatcher was the most popular choice. Madonna, Mother Teresa, Golda Meir—the list revealed something obvious: There has been no Rosa Parks of women's rights in recent years, no splendid average person whose indignity summed up injustice.

Now there are real women to hang the issues and the anger on. Mention Anita Hill and there is still an adrenaline rush. "I thought I'd stop feeling angry when it was over," one woman said of the hearings, which Jay Leno likes to say could have wiped out the federal deficit if they had aired on pay-per-view. "But I'm still mad."

And why not? History repeats herself. Many of the members of the Senate treated Professor Hill's accusations the way the officials at Dow Corning treated the pain of women whose implants had gone haywire. Hysterics. Complainers. Crybabies.

Women who get beaten up by their husbands can tell you about this phenomenon. They know the moments when their eye is slowly turning indigo and their old man says, "You made me do it." "Why did you stick around?" people asked Anita Hill. "Why did you go there?" they asked Ms. Washington, who was believed, and Patricia Bowman, who was not. The good guys of America should be tired of this blame-the-victim stuff, which assumes that any woman with half a brain knows that her male counterpart is the functional equivalent of a loaded gun.

People have been predicting the death of feminism for years now, but feminism isn't dead. Like any distance runner with a long way to go, it was just getting a second wind. Now there are more real people to make the political personal, which is to make it real.

Rape victims have stepped forward. Women who feel that they've been maimed by big business and big medicine are speaking out. And Professor Hill has come to stand in many minds not only for sexual harassment but for courage, dignity, and a refusal to move to the back of the gender bus. I bet she'll be near the top of the Barnard list come September. I wonder how much her example encouraged Desiree Washington not to back off but to move forward.

MS. PRESIDENT

April 19, 1992

Donna Karan, the only fashion designer who seems to recognize the existence of hips in her clientele, perhaps because she owns a pair herself, recently ran an arresting series of magazine advertisements.

In one, the woman in the pin-striped suit is standing behind a bunting-draped lectern. In another, she is sitting on the back of a convertible amid grim guys with headsets, confetti dappling her hair. In a third, she is raising her right hand, a handsome man at her side, while a judge holds the Bible. Congratulations, Ms. President.

The model looks scarcely old enough to meet the constitutional requirements and too décolleté to meet the public ones. She's accepting the tribute of a grateful nation with a lace bra peeking out from beneath her half-buttoned blouse, fashion's current Madonna/whore obsession. The slogan is "In Women We Trust," but there's something slightly camp about the whole thing.

Camp is how the nation still sees it as well.

You've got to wonder, approaching a new century, when America will begin to take seriously the idea of being led by a woman. The concept heretofore has always been presented as a cross between a futuristic fantasy and a sitcom premise. Cue the laugh track.

We've heard the rationales. We've heard that there are not enough terrific women in the pipeline, that with so few in the House and the Senate it is inevitable that most of the major players are men.

There are about to be two problems with the pipeline excuse. One is that a record number of women are running for seats in Congress this year. The second is the dirty little secret that has suddenly become so apparent: there are not that many terrific men in the pipeline, either.

In a recently published study called *Women in Power*, two psychologists talked to twenty-five of the country's most powerful female elected officials. They found that many of them did not run for office until after their families were well launched, foreclosing the Wunderkind status and power-base building that accrue to men like Bill Clinton or Al Gore. They found that many of them were gingerly negotiating the contradictions between traditional notions of leadership and traditional notions of femininity.

But many had been told from childhood that they could do anything, and they still believed it. Given the chance, maybe they could convince us, too.

Consider Ann Richards, who became famous for her convention speech about how good ol' George Bush was born with a silver foot in his mouth—and who, God bless her, has no dirty linen left unaired after a snake's belly of a gubernatorial challenge. Governor of Texas, a biiig important state. Smart, can-do, and as charming as a full moon on an autumn night. Truth is that if Ms. Richards is not soon mentioned as a national candidate, it won't be because of her competence. It will be because of her chromosomes.

I've heard women wonder aloud about when the idea of a woman president will be something more than an occasion for gags about the First Man. Opportunities for women have expanded so much that those gender deserts in which change is scarce water have become more wrenching.

This month the American Catholic bishops released another draft of their pastoral letter on women's concerns. It begins well, calling sexism a sin, and then ends, sadly, with the Church's continuing theology of exclusion, its reaffirmation of the priesthood as the exclusive preserve of men. "This constant practice constitutes a tradition which witnesses to the mind of Christ and is therefore normative," the letter reads.

I could inveigh here against the sheer foolishness of any system that excludes at least half of its finest potential leaders. But the murmurings about a woman president (as well as women priests) are not only about expanding what seems to be a shockingly shallow applicant pool.

They are questions about how we as women are valued, and how we learn to value ourselves. Neither political nor church leaders seem to adequately appreciate that a system that, by custom or covert agreement, considers women unsuitable for its highest positions sends them a message: You are subordinate clauses in the world's history.

No rationale can obscure that message. When our daughters ask why they may never see a woman president or a woman priest, we have no good answers for them. That is because there are none.

NOT ABOUT
BREASTS

January 19, 1992

"I am not a piece of machinery for which they manufactured a new part. I am real. I am somebody's mother and somebody's wife."

Because the plastic surgeon was using a local anesthetic, Mariann Hopkins heard his exclamation when he saw what was inside her. She heard him call for an anesthesiologist. She heard him say, "Both implants have ruptured." And then they put her under.

In the beginning I thought the furor about breast implants was about breasts. This is convenient. As soon as we begin to talk about vanity, sexuality, and self-image, attention is diverted from the real issue.

This is not about breasts. This is about business as usual and Dow Corning, a company that manufactures silicone implants and has sold millions of them.

We know that unsatisfactory products are sold all the time. But finding a split seam in your new suit and hearing a doctor talk about teasing stray bits of silicone out of your chest wall are two different things. It would be grand to know that those who manu-facture body parts hold themselves to a higher standard than the makers of acrylic sweaters.

We have ample evidence to know this is not true. We have women whose reproductive organs were removed when they were barely past puberty because their own mothers took a synthetic estrogen during pregnancy that caused cancer in their daugh-ters. We have women whose reproductive organs were maimed by an intrauterine device.

We have lived with a negative standard—not unsafe—instead of the affirmative standard we deserve. Some makers of diethyl-stilbestrol, or DES, still insist there is doubt about whether their useless product caused cancer. The makers of the Dalkon shield collapsed into the safe and sheltering arms of bankruptcy still insisting that their device, which caused infection, infertility, and even death, was safe and effective.

Safe and effective: that's what Dow Corning says about silicone implants, even as the Food and Drug Administration has declared a moratorium on their use. Every day there are new allegations: that company officials misrepresented data to the Food and Drug Administration, that they suppressed results that would be detri-mental to their bottom line, that they did inadequate testing. Some plastic surgeons asked about research years ago. "I assured them, with crossed fingers, that Dow Corning too had an active study underway," a marketing executive wrote.

That was part of a memo that was used when Mrs. Hopkins brought suit. She hired her lawyers with one condition: she said she would never settle out of court. She had spent years thinking that there was no link between her painful and debilitating con-nective-tissue disease and the implants that she received after a mastectomy.

And then she began to hear that there were documents that indicated otherwise but that had been sealed as part of out-of-court settlements. And she got mad. And even. According to Mrs.

Hopkins, Dow Corning's lawyers offered her almost $2 million just before closing arguments in her case. She refused. The jury awarded her $7.3 million.

Most of that was in punitive damages, although it will be a long, long time before she sees any money because the company is appealing. But she's satisfied. Her case is part of the public debate, and six ordinary people sent a message to Dow Corning: You did a very, very bad thing.

There are many women who have silicone implants and think they're terrific. They constitute the majority, although no one knows if they will have problems in years to come. Dow Corning likes to argue that women have a right to make their own decisions about implants, a freedom-of-choice argument that is a good sell.

But I'm not buying from Dow Corning right now. Women have a right to implants—a right to safe ones, rigorously tested with the best interests of people placed before the bottom line.

"As long as we don't make a fuss we don't get anything better," said Mrs. Hopkins. We must make a fuss, and the Food and Drug Administration, which has acted laudably in this case, must stay with us every step of the way, so that dangers are recognized before the damage is done. We are not machinery, to be tinkered with and then patched together when it turns out the parts don't work. But that is how we have been treated for too long a time.

CONTRADICTIONS

January 8, 1992

Videotape confers a peculiar kind of immortality. The parents of Major Marie Rossi can watch their daughter, alive as anything, tell the world how she feels about what she does. In a jaunty camouflage hat, she stands in the desert and tells the cameras what some of us were saying in print: that national defense is sex-blind. "What I am doing is no greater or less than the man who is flying next to me," she said, as pundits were opining the same on the home front.

But we were only operating word processors while Major Rossi was flying a Chinook chopper for the Army, and the day after the cease-fire the chopper crashed. She was buried in Arlington Cemetery, where a memorial to women in America's wars is planned. Rewind. Play. "We thought it was pretty neat that three women were going to be across the border before the rest of the battalion," Major Rossi, forever upbeat, tells CNN.

Fast forward.

It's been a year since we went to war in the Persian Gulf. Most of the veterans came home to their bases or to their civilian jobs. The people who help the homeless say they're seeing some of them in shelters or on the streets. And some came home to verdant places like Arlington.

Major Rossi was perhaps the best known of the casualties, a kind of poster figure in that war which redefined the role of military women. At banquets and memorial ceremonies, her parents have become accustomed to having her come alive on tape, her open face and matter-of-fact manner summing up all that we think of as particularly American.

"She was a very compassionate person," says Gertrude Rossi, remembering her daughter's last letter, dated the day before she died, describing with empathy the prisoners she was transporting, barefoot and ragged, boys and old men.

It has been a year of gender wars in America; at no other time have the motives, mind-set, roles, and relationships of men and women been as thoroughly dissected and debated. The problem in these debates has been a classic one—a yen for simplicity, for no contradictions, no complications. A philosophical framework that long ago outlived its usefulness. Either you are a good girl or a bad one: no middle ground. Either you are a victim or a strong woman, not both. Either you are a soldier or a mother. Choose.

So many of us have chosen lives of seeming contradictions, at odds with the old ways. I remember mentioning the baby-sitter in a column once and receiving outraged letters from readers who could not understand how anyone who could write feelingly of her children would hire help with their care. When did those people think I was writing? In the checkout line at the supermarket?

It came as a surprise to me, looking back, to see that I began the year 1990 by considering women in combat in Panama. (Remember Panama?) And I began 1991 by considering women in combat in Saudi Arabia. The good news is that at the beginning of 1992 the question of women in combat has gone back to being a philosophical issue.

The philosophy will inevitably be shaped by Major Rossi and others like her. Like them, so many of us said matter-of-factly that women should do the jobs that they could do. But there was no doubt that it was a stretch, for those simultaneously feminist and pacifist, to fight for the right of women to freely choose what we abhorred.

There is accomplishment contained in this description of Major Rossi: First Female Combat Commander to Fly into Battle. There is infinite sadness that the description is on her headstone. Equal access to body bags: that is a tough one to argue from the heart.

Some of us were afraid to argue what we really felt, that the world would be better served if we all internalized those traits that have been seen, for whatever reason, as female. If we stopped thinking physical aggression was the obvious way to settle things. If we stopped seeing talk as weak and wimpy. If world politics became less a test of manhood and more a matter of coexistence.

I remember reading what Major Rossi's husband said at her funeral, as powerful a contrast as I have ever heard. "I prayed that guidance be given to her so that she could command the company, so she could lead her troops in battle," he said. "And I prayed to the Lord to take care of my sweet little wife."

THE GLASS
HALF EMPTY

November 22, 1990

My daughter is two years old today. She is something like me,
only better. Or at least that is what I like to think. If personalities
had colors, hers would be red.

Little by little, in the twenty years between my eighteenth birthday and her second one, I had learned how to live in the world.
The fact that women were now making 67 cents for every dollar a
man makes—well, it was better than 1970, wasn't it, when we
were making only 59 cents? The constant stories about the
underrepresentation of women, on the tenure track in the film
industry, in government, everywhere, had become commonplace. The rape cases. The sexual harassment stories. The
demeaning comments. Life goes on. Where's your sense of
humor?

Learning to live in the world meant seeing the glass half full.
Ann Richards was elected governor of Texas instead of a good ol'
boy who said that if rape was inevitable, you should relax and
enjoy it. The police chief of Houston is a pregnant woman who

has a level this-is-my-job look and a maternity uniform with stars on the shoulder. There are so many opportunities unheard of when I was growing up.

And then I had a daughter and suddenly I saw the glass half empty. And all the rage I thought had cooled, all those how-dare-you-treat-us-like-that days, all of it comes back when I look at her, and especially when I hear her say to her brothers, "Me too."

When I look at my sons, it is within reason to imagine all the world's doors open to them. Little by little some will close, as their individual capabilities and limitations emerge. But no one is likely to look at them and mutter: "I'm not sure a man is right for a job at this level. Doesn't he have a lot of family responsibilities?"

Every time a woman looks at her daughter and thinks, She can be anything, she knows in her heart, from experience, that it's a lie. Looking at this little girl, I see it all, the old familiar ways of a world that still loves Barbie. Girls aren't good at math, dear. He needs the money more than you, sweetheart; he's got a family to support. Honey—this diaper's dirty.

It is like looking through a telescope. Over the years I learned to look through the end that showed things small and manageable. This is called a sense of proportion. And then I turned the telescope around, and all the little tableaux rushed at me, vivid as ever. That's called reality.

We soothe ourselves with the gains that have been made. There are many role models. Role models are women who exist—and are photographed often—to make other women feel better about the fact that there aren't really enough of us anywhere, except in the lowest-paying jobs. A newspaper editor said to me not long ago, with no hint of self-consciousness, "I'd love to run your column, but we already run Ellen Goodman." Not only was there a quota; there was a quota of one.

My daughter is ready to leap into the world, as though life were chicken soup and she a delighted noodle. The work of Professor Carol Gilligan of Harvard suggests that sometime after the age of eleven this will change, that even this lively little girl will pull back, shrink, that her constant refrain will become "I don't know." Professor Gilligan says the culture sends a message: "Keep quiet and notice the absence of women and say nothing." A smart thirteen-year-old said to me last week, "Boys don't like it if you answer too much in class."

Maybe someday, years from now, my daughter will come home and say, "Mother, at college my professor acted as if my studies were an amusing hobby and at work the man who runs my department puts his hand on my leg and to compete with the man who's in the running for my promotion who makes more than I do I can't take time to have a relationship but he has a wife and two children and I'm smarter and it doesn't make any difference and some guy tried to jump me after our date last night." And what am I supposed to say to her?

I know?

You'll get used to it?

No. Today is her second birthday and she has made me see fresh this two-tiered world, a world that, despite all our nonsense about post-feminism, continues to offer less respect and less opportunity for women than it does for men. My friends and I have learned to live with it, but my little girl deserves better. She has given me my anger back, and I intend to use it well.

That is her gift to me today. Some birthday I will return it to her, because she is going to need it.

ABOUT THE AUTHOR

ANNA QUINDLEN joined *The New York Times* in 1977, and has been a general assignment reporter, City Hall reporter, and the paper's deputy metropolitan editor. She is the third woman to write a column for the Op-Ed page. That column, "Public & Private," appears in *The New York Times* and in newspapers throughout the country and became the book *Thinking Out Loud*. It is the third column she has written for the paper. From 1981 to 1983 she wrote "About New York," and in 1986 she created the column "Life in the 30s"; a collection of those essays was published by Random House as *Living Out Loud*. In addition to her best-selling novel, *Object Lessons*, she has written a children's book, *The Tree That Came to Stay*.

A 1974 graduate of Barnard College and a member of the college's Board of Trustees, she has been awarded Columbia University's Meyer Berger prize for the best writing about New York and the University Medal of Excellence. Her work had also been honored by the Associated Press, Women in Communications, and she was named by *Glamour* magazine as one of the ten outstanding women of 1991. She was the winner of the Pulitzer Prize for commentary in 1992.